What people are saying about

Tending Sacred Ground

This collection of insights on parenting is a joy. The nuggets of wisdom come in an easily absorbable size, are gently offered, and nudge us to rethink attitudes and interactions we take for granted as parents, grandparents, teachers, coaches, and family members. Each nugget brings a story and moves us another step toward grace and respect. Pamela Haines shows how warmth can infuse respect, bringing us adults closer to our best selves, and building a world in which children are free to play, think, make mistakes, and learn without shame or blame. With short, pungent passages containing fresh insights about what love entails when we're with the young people we care about, it's an ideal bedside table book. In five or ten minutes, we can go to sleep having set our sights again on what it means to truly care in this topsy-turvy world.

Patty Wipfler, Founder, Hand in Hand Parenting

The heart of *Tending Sacred Ground* is an invitation to be present as we call on deep wells of respect—for our own parents, for our children, and for ourselves. Pamela Haines is a great storyteller because she's also an excellent *noticer*—of herself, her own children and others, the work and joy of parenting, and our condition as human beings. In the spirit of the best kind of parenting book, this one shows the way with stories about celebration and challenge, stumbles and openings, growing and revelations alongside our children.

Melinda Wenner Bradley, Coordinator, Philadelphia Quaker Youth Religious Life

T0099360

Straight advice can be very welcome to parents wondering if it's time to start their baby on spinach. But in the more complicated questions of care and upbringing, the beauty of a story is that it doesn't expect obedience or resistance—it raises questions. Pamela sometimes offers us wise counsel, but I was more struck by her uncertainties and the number of direct or implied questions on almost every page. A great beauty of this book is the way it treats children as moral agents who have the right to their own views and satisfactions. Pamela urges us to recognize that they can be our teachers too—if we let them.

John Lampen, Author of *The Peace Kit, The Worship Kit* and *Peaceful Inside*

This book is a gift to parents. It raises parenting to the spiritual realm that—though seldom acknowledged—it is. The forty reflections are of a parent seeking to do her best as she lives with and guides her children. Two recurring themes make this book so helpful to parents. One is the author's straightforward acknowledgment of her own feelings, negative as well as positive. Another is her respect for the feelings of children. As parents recognize themselves in the segments of family life, this book will help them to deepen their own spiritual journeys.

Harriet Heath Ph.D, Convenor, Quaker Parenting Initiative

QUAKER QUICKS

Tending Sacred Ground

Respectful Parenting

QUAKER QUICKS

Tending Sacred Ground

Respectful Parenting

Pamela Haines

CHRISTIAN ALTERNATIVE
BOOKS

Winchester, UK
Washington, USA

JOHN HUNT PUBLISHING

First published by Christian Alternative Books, 2022
Christian Alternative Books is an imprint of John Hunt Publishing Ltd.,
No. 3 East St., Alresford, Hampshire SO24 9EE, UK
office@jhpbooks.com
www.johnhuntpublishing.com
www.christian-alternative.com

For distributor details and how to order please visit the 'Ordering' section on our website.

Text copyright: Pamela Haines 2021

ISBN: 978 1 80341 088 3
978 1 80341 089 0 (ebook)
Library of Congress Control Number: 2021951703

A CIP catalogue record for this book is available from the British Library.

Design: Stuart Davies

UK: Printed and bound by CPI Group (UK) Ltd, Croydon, CR0 4YY
US: Printed and bound by Thomson-Shore, 7300 West Joy Road, Dexter, MI 48130

We operate a distinctive and ethical publishing philosophy in all areas of our business, from our global network of authors to production and worldwide distribution.

Contents

Previous books

Toward a Right Relationship with Finance: Debt, Interest, Growth, and Security 978-9768142887
Money and Soul: Quaker Faith and Practice and the Economy 978-1789040892
That Clear and Certain Sound: Finding Solid Ground in Perilous Times 978-1789047653
Alive in this World 978-9768273260

The quotes at the beginning of each chapter come from *Faith and Practice, Philadelphia Yearly Meeting of the Religious Society of Friends,* paraphrased there from materials contained in *Quaker Epistles from Philadelphia and the Jerseys,* 1694 and 1695.

Preface

Tending Sacred Ground: Respectful Parenting

We lay with our mother on our backs on the grass-filled lot where our community played baseball, looking up at the night sky. She pointed out individual stars and constellations and told the stories of their names.

When we were building an addition to our house, everyone had a job, based on their age and abilities. As an 11-year-old, I was too young to be trusted to pound finishing nails cleanly into ridged wall shingles, so I worked with my grandfather on putting up the under-shingles. I was expected to be competent to measure, space and nail, and I did my job with pleasure and pride.

Our Quaker congregation always had fifteen minutes of singing around the piano before settling into the quiet expectant waiting of worship. I was learning piano, and one day the person who usually played wasn't there, and it turned out that I had the most experience of the gathered group. As a pre-teen, the prospect terrified me, but the community's willingness to accept and make use of the abilities I could bring to the group was a gift.

One April, when winter was stubbornly hanging on and spring couldn't seem to get a grip, my mother decided that we needed to help out, and she organized a "Welcome Sweet Springtime" party. We cut sheets from the big roll of brown paper she always had, painted the most spring-like pictures we could imagine and hung them all over our big open downstairs room. We baked and decorated. We sang. We manifested spring in every way we knew how, and had to believe that our joyous celebration played its small part in helping to break the grip of that cold winter.

Since Quakerism isn't a creedal religion, we didn't get told what to believe. So, the process by which we absorbed what it meant to be part of this community was a subtle, and often uneven, one. Of course, much of it was by observation.

I can call to mind just three of the lessons from Sunday School. The most vivid was the year my mother taught our class. Her theme was children from around the world. Every week she would read us a story from a different part of the world and we would draw — and probably talk about the story, though it is the drawing that I remember. Then we would make a collage on an enormous sheet of cardboard that represented our experience of that story. When the theme was Japan, we learned some haiku which was included in the collage. Together, over the course of that year, we constructed a great cardboard book, held together with big round book rings, each sheet a visual reminder of our shared exploration of the world. We were learners, artists, co-creators, active participants in a community that spanned the globe.

Then, when I was thirteen, our Sunday School teacher started the year off by asking us what was on our hearts and minds. This was one of the most significant moments of my childhood. No one had ever asked me that question before, at least not with such a clear intention of accepting and respecting whatever I said. We all knew this man's gentleness and fierce integrity; there was no doubt that he meant what he said. It was like finding a bubbling spring of fresh water. It was also a little scary. Would I dare let out into the light things I had been holding tight inside me all those years? But where else would I ever have a better opportunity?

Finally, when I was in high school, we spent our Sunday School class time with a series of adults from the meeting. I think it was because they couldn't find one person who was prepared to carry the entire load, but it turned out to be a wonderful year of getting fuller access to a handful of grown-ups we saw every Sunday but knew little about. People shared stories of their faith journey, bringing us in to what mattered to them in their lives.

All these experiences nourished the soil of my own parenting. Raising our children was a never-ending process of tending sacred ground—which I captured as best I knew how along the way in the reflections that follow. I came to this work with all my struggles and blind spots, blessed by the gifts that had been given to me as a child, along with a growing understanding of the power of listening that I gained as a young adult.

My Quaker training helped to center me as a parent in seeking for integrity at the heart of my interactions, holding my assumptions and behavior up to the light, and responding to the divine spark in those around me. It was a guide along that rocky road that all parents travel, wishing more for our children than we are able to give, full of regrets, all doing our best.

* * *

My four-year-old grandson and I lie on our backs in the snow looking up through the bare tree branches to the sky above. We've taken a break from play to drink in the immensity and the beauty of the heavens. It is a sacred moment, made all the more precious because I am following his lead. Could I have done more, I wonder, to cultivate these opportunities with my own children? Was I too matter-of-fact, too reluctant to impose my sense of the sacred on them? I have to believe that it was enough.

Foreword

To guide us in our relationships with our children, Pamela Haines tells lots of stories—just as Jesus did. Straight advice can be very welcome to parents wondering if it's time to start their baby on spinach. But in the more complicated questions of care and upbringing, the beauty of a story is that it doesn't expect obedience or resistance—it raises questions. Pamela sometimes offers us wise counsel. But I was more struck by her uncertainties, by the number of direct or implied questions on almost every page of this book.

Jesus' stories have the same quality. "What do you think?" he says. "There's a fellow with two sons. He says to one, 'Son, go down today and work in my vineyard.' 'No way!' the lad replies; but later he feels sorry and goes. The father says the same to the other son. 'Sure, Dad!' he answers—but he never turns up."

Matthew uses this story in his gospel to buttress his argument with the rabbis of his day. But if we put on one side the original context and culture, it starts to ask us other questions. Does a father have the right to command service from his children? What would happen if we made a similar demand on our own children? If the second boy is at fault, is it for preferring to go off on his own business (which may be important) or simply for fobbing Dad off with a lie? Are we expected to approve the first son's compliance? The story looks short and simple but it pulls us into complicated family issues and leaves us to work out our own conclusions. Many of Pamela's examples have the same effect on me—not least because she shares her own reaction to each situation so honestly.

The great beauty of this book is the way it treats children as moral agents who have the right to their own views and satisfactions. She notes how they can be dependent and

4

independent by turns many times each day, so they sometimes need freedom, sometimes guidance, and occasionally coercion. Pamela urges us to recognize that they can be our teachers too — if we let them.

I'd like to share an experience of my own with you. Some years ago, I used to assist voluntarily in a local school. Its future was in doubt, and the ambitious headmaster was determined to save it; but his tools were blame and bullying. One day two teachers were ill, so he had to teach a class himself. I was helping a girl of six with her sums, and from two classrooms away we could hear him yelling at his class. I was feeling very angry and disgusted with him, when the little girl looked up and, without a trace of fear at his anger, said to me: "Mr. M isn't very happy today, is he?" I am still grateful years later for this lesson in compassion. John Lampen

John is the author of three books for younger teenagers, *The Peace Kit*, *The Worship Kit* and the novel *Hester and Sophie*; also, *Peaceful Inside* for children ages 5 to 7.

Introduction

A Tribute to Mothers

We were ordinary mothers on an ordinary block in West Philadelphia, taking advantage of the leisurely sociability of a block party to talk about—what else?—our children. We had ordinary problems—how to decide about schools, how to work and still have time for the children, how to help our teenagers make choices and live with consequences.

Yet there was something about that conversation that touched me, that has stayed with me all these weeks. I think it was the love and strength that I saw. And it was a glimpse of how very much we have in common.

Regardless of our age, our background, our color, our beliefs, we are all doing the very best we can for our children. We are all struggling in less-than-ideal circumstances (at least everyone I know), making compromises in our lives for their sakes. We are calling on resources of love and strength that we may never have known we had in order to do this job. We all deserve so much more recognition than we get. This has been one of the great gifts of motherhood to me. I feel part of a continuous thread stretching beyond my neighborhood, to neighborhoods all over the world. And the thread stretches in time as well, back through the years to other mothers, doing just the same work, hoping just the same hopes, calling on just the same unimagined resources.

I treasure this glimpse of belonging to such a strong, loving group. And I wonder why it comes only in glimpses. I'm pretty sure I'm not the only one who often feels like I'm doing this alone. Even with a husband (and I'm a great fan of fathers!), even with relatives, even with a neighborhood, school or church community, it's easy to feel alone in the day-to-day work of being a mother.

A parent leader for whom I have the greatest respect once said that our experience of isolation as parents may stem from the fact that we don't often speak of our deep love for our children, our delight in them. Thus we are not communicating fully who we are and what is important to us.

We're hungry for a chance to talk about our children—and there's lots to say. The complaints, the dilemmas, the near disasters come first. They're what's on top, and we need to talk about them. But the hard times are not the whole story, and, somehow, it's harder to tell of our love. We're embarrassed, we're ambivalent, we're protective, we're shy. But our love for our children is so good, so deep, so central to our hopes for a better world. The more of it that can be made visible, the better off all of us will be.

1

Cultivating Respect

Let us renounce for ourselves the power of any person over any other.

Drawing from the well

A friend and I were talking about her new husband's relationship to her six-year-old daughter. "He just wants discipline. Things would go so much better if he would play with her sometimes, but he never does. His mother never played with him, and he won't hear a word against her."

This story, about a man I'd never met, touched a chord. I've always resonated with loyalty, and there was something about his stubbornness that I appreciated. I know we're never going to help people change by criticizing those they love; clearly, he knew that too. And I think he had an important understanding about oppression. His mother was struggling to do well by her loved ones in a society that lacked some basic respect for her and her family. In a situation where respect is so grossly lacking from the outside, it makes perfect sense for a perceptive and loving child to take a stand, holding up that respect and demanding it from others.

We have to start with recognizing the goodness of our parents, and giving them credit for the job they did. Though some had to struggle more than others, and their struggles took very different forms, they all raised their families under adverse circumstances and without adequate support. Though some were more successful than others, they all did the very best they could figure out, and this reality needs to be the starting place.

If we can give full respect to the past it can stand by itself, leaving us free to move on. I appreciate this good son's fierce loyalty, but I wish that he did not feel compelled to replicate his mother's parenting style in honor of all her love and hard work. How might he combine that respect with the possibility of something new? I wondered if my friend could ask him, "Can you imagine what it would have been like if your mother had had time to play with you?" "Yes," she said eagerly. "Yes, I think that might work."

Another friend was puzzling over her daughter's lack of consideration for others. "I try so hard to model being considerate of her. I listen to her, take her wishes into account, bend over backwards to help her get things the way she wants them. I thought that if I did that for her, she would just naturally do it for others. What's wrong?"

I didn't know what to say, because that's been my philosophy too: If you model thoughtfulness toward your children, they will naturally learn to be thoughtful. When the insight came to me, it was very simple: my friend was doing a terrific job modeling consideration *for her child*, but not *for herself*. The message her child was getting was that the needs of the other person in the interaction were not important. Of course. No wonder she wasn't in the habit of being considerate.

What to do? Either you put yourself first and wield your adult authority to require the children to conform to your wishes, or you put the children first and they grow up into inconsiderate, ungrateful brutes. If we have any glimmer of a sense that children are complete human beings who deserve to be treated with respect, then this seems like a terrible pair of choices.

If we think, however, of modeling respect for all the human beings in our environment, *our children and ourselves included*, then we can find a third way. While the best response to any given situation may not be clear, at least we are on solid ground. For some of us, the struggle may be to think of the children first—even though they are squarely in the way of our own wants. For others, who would sacrifice anything for our children, the challenge may be trying to imagine what we want for ourselves and going for it, knowing that any suffering they feel will be outweighed by the value of seeing us treat ourselves with respect.

This job of parenting calls on deep wells of respect—for our own parents, for our children, and for ourselves. They will thrive on experiencing us giving all that respect. After all, we're their models for what it is like to be an adult.

Manners

I got a thrill one day when I heard my four-year-old, in response to a request from one of his friends, say, "I would be glad to do that for you." I recognized my own words and intonation. He had learned that response from me!

It can be frightening sometimes to see how directly we can pass things on to our children—our less than rational or attractive fears, intolerance, body language, tones of voice. I've experienced this before with dismay, so it was wonderful to get such clear evidence that I'm passing on positive qualities as well. Overhearing that sentence also strengthened the case for my belief that the only real way to teach "good manners" to children is to model them.

I believe in manners. I think that "please" and "thank you" are like oil that lubricates the moving parts in people's interactions. We often don't interact smoothly, there's often friction, and a little oil can help a lot. Maybe it's because I see good manners this way—as an expression of thoughtfulness rather than a set of "do's and don'ts" or an obligatory social code—that I'm skeptical of teaching them as rules.

There's no question that children can learn rules, memorize when to apply them and have that behavior reinforced by praise or punishment. But if my goal is to teach thoughtfulness about other human beings, then a set of rules is not enough. They need to see thoughtfulness in action in thousands of different situations. And they need to experience thoughtfulness directed toward themselves.

When we think about good manners, we usually focus on children being polite to their elders. We may also think of adults treating each other with civility rather than rudeness. But how often do we think of adults being polite to children—making requests with a respectful "please," remembering each "thank you," prefacing each interruption with an "excuse me"?

What if all adults made a point of being polite, in the most thoughtful way they know how, not only with other adults, but with their children and the children around them as well? Would we still need to teach manners?

We can help our children by letting them know how lack of thoughtfulness affects *us*. ("When that person acts that way, I just feel so ___! I wish instead that they would say ___. It seems like a little thing, but it makes such a big difference.") This may be hardest to communicate when the problem is *their* lack of thoughtfulness in our regard. When my children start issuing commands, without any semblance of politeness ("Give me a glass of water") I am incensed. That is the point at which I want to drill good manners into their obnoxious little skulls. But before responding, I try to remember how many times they get commands issued at them. If that's the model they see of how powerful people get results, then it's not surprising that they copy it.

With this in mind, I'm more able to talk calmly about how much more willing I feel to respond to a request rather than to an order. My youngest can get very stubborn and I don't want to make a big issue out of it, so sometimes I just say, "Did I hear you say please pour me a glass of water?" He'll usually nod, and I'll smile and hug him and say, "That's what I *thought* I heard." The nod is all I need in order to feel thought about—and the machinery of human interaction moves smoothly again.

Nobody likes a test

I was in a car with a group of children and one of them, full of recently acquired knowledge about hawks, was testing the rest of us. "What is the largest hawk? What is the fastest hawk?" I noted my growing feeling of irritation, all out of proportion to the innocence of this boy's pleasure in his new knowledge.

Now I wouldn't mind a request for the information I have about hawks because he would really like to know, or even an inquiry about whether I know much on that subject. Each of those is a genuine desire for new knowledge—worlds apart from asking, *with knowledge in hand*, to see how I rate.

I hate to be tested—and oral testing is by far the worst. The many times when I know the answer to the test question don't make up for the stupidity I feel when the space after the question grows longer and I just can't find the answer, or know that what I'm about to say to break that silence is probably wrong.

Maybe there are some people who like being tested—people who make a vocation of learning the right answers to questions, or people who are knowledgeable or skilled enough in one particular area that they welcome the chance to show off. But I would also guess that I'm in the majority, that most of us would exert some effort to avoid being put in that position.

All of which brings me to the subject of testing children. Quite apart from what goes on in school, we parents do an enormous amount of testing, and we start very young. "Who is that sitting across the table?" "What color is this?" "How many fingers do I have up?" "What is eight and four?" "What animal is in that picture?" We do it so much that we don't even notice. Yet I can't imagine that they like to be tested any more than we do.

What if we never, ever asked a question whose answer we already knew? Some people might worry that the children would never learn, or that we'd never know if they were learning or not. But if you talk in conversation about colors, about people's names and names of things, children will pick them up just as they do the rest of the language. Sooner or later we'll just discover that they know, without ever having to test.

If we're really desperate to know if a child knows, we can always ask: "Do you know what this is called?" That's a question whose answer we don't know. (Of course, if they respond with an unadorned "yes" or "no", then we should be satisfied because our question has been answered.)

We can also ask if a child would *like* to be tested—another question to which we may not know the answer. I have a son who actually enjoys answering math questions, and so long as he's the one who decides, the testing can be fun for both of us. (He's also very clear about when he's done.)

Adults rarely test each other in normal conversation. In a way, it's a simple matter of respect, of treating children as we would any other human being. So—what if we never asked a question whose answer we already knew? What a question that is!

On children's love and grief

It can be scary to see how *deeply* our children feel. Caring deeply is such a set-up for getting hurt. It's so easy to identify with them and want to protect. If I've experienced that kind of hurt myself and never want to experience it again, I can't stand seeing them set themselves up for it.

The obvious protection is to counsel them not to care too much, particularly when they're pouring it out on something that seems silly or insignificant. If they're heart-broken over the breaking of a cheap little plastic toy, I want to explain why it's not that big a deal. I'm glad to warn them against getting deeply attached to a bug that's bound to die, one I would have a hard time imagining loving anyway.

But if I listen to my words in those "silly" or "insignificant" cases, is this what I really want to communicate to my children? "Don't hope, don't love; you'll just get hurt." I don't think so.

The problem is not in the caring, which is good, but in knowing what to do with the pain, which can be excruciating.

For "big" losses, we're allowed to grieve. When a loved one dies, everyone would agree that "it's better to have loved and lost than to never have loved at all." We expect the huge outbursts of grief at these times; we even worry if they *don't* come. We just think that "little" losses should be able to be handled differently. But they're really just the same. It's not the size or value or importance of the object, but the *depth of our loving* that brings the depth of our grief.

So, I try to withhold judgment and just encourage that love, knowing there may be tears down the road. And I try not to be taken aback at the depth of the grief.

When my eldest's little tiny itsy-bitsy shrimp died (they weren't as large as houseflies), he was absolutely heart-broken. I remembered all this good thinking, took a deep breath and decided to take it as seriously as the death of a dearest friend. And he cried and cried and cried. I think it was my attitude—that this was real and important and big—that allowed him to grieve so fully. Each time he stopped crying, I'd test whether he was really done by calling his attention once more to the fact that the shrimp really were dead, and saying what a *good* lover he was and how much I loved him for that, and he would cry some more.

After about half an hour, he seemed to be done but still wanted to be close to me, so I took him to my meeting (for which I was late by now), still operating on the decision to take this situation totally seriously. He stayed close and sad for a little while, but pretty soon was ready to turn his attention elsewhere. Since then, when the shrimp have come up in conversation, his tone has been very matter of fact. And he hasn't stopped giving his heart away to little animals—so something had been right.

I'll probably never know how much he was grieving for the shrimp (which I, from my adult perspective, still can't believe he loved that much), and how much he was using my unusually open and accepting attitude to cry about other accumulated griefs that hadn't had a place to come out. But I do know that I want to give my children the chance to grieve about *everything* that they love and lose—to keep them willing to love as fully and deeply as they know how.

Speaking truth about home life

A mother brought her almost two-year-old to our parent and toddler group full of hard stories of life at home. Her husband, badly overworked, never even-tempered at the best of times, had been yelling, slamming doors, picking fights—blowing off steam big time. Now I know what a good man he is, how much he loves his wife and daughter, how much they love him, how safe they are from real danger. I wasn't worried. But I also know that this was hard on all of them. While the little girl was greeting friends and finding playthings, I listened to the mom— just giving her a chance to tell about her morning and cry a little bit about how hard it was.

Then it occurred to me that the daughter had had a similar morning, and perhaps had her own story to tell. I sat down on the floor beside her to play, and when she said something about her dad, I said, in a conversational tone, that I heard he'd been yelling and slamming doors that morning. She nodded and said something about the kitchen, which her mom interpreted as the place of the loudest fight. I said it sounded as if her dad was having a hard time—mad about having to work so much, and mad about not being able to be with his beloved daughter. She said something about mad. I said we all get mad sometimes. I get mad, she gets mad, her mom and dad get mad, and it helps when someone can listen and not worry.

She didn't seem to have anything more to say on the topic, and after playing a while longer I moved on to other people. I felt that there was more here than met the eye, but didn't see anything else to do. Only later, as I was talking about it with a friend, did I think how helpful such an interaction would have been to *me* as a child.

What would it have been like if an adult who knew and liked my parents had chatted with me about what it was like living with them? They might have mentioned how difficult it was for either of my parents to say directly what they wanted. They might have commented that it could be hard when you knew your mother or father was angry but they pretended everything was fine. They might have wondered out loud what a child would do, in such a loving family, with the unloving feelings she must have sometimes, as everybody does.

Even if they had done no more than that, it would have been a great service. Loving my parents, and trusting them to interpret the world for me, I was at a loss for how to make sense of some of what went on. When things don't have an explanation you can understand, what can you do besides assume that everything is out of control, or that somehow it's your fault?

Having another adult who cared about my parents see my reality and frame it in a way that I could understand would have been an enormous relief. Letting me know that it was okay to have the feelings that I had might have transformed my experience of childhood.

I think we rarely take this step with other people's children. It feels like intruding on other people's very private affairs, invading the sanctity of the home, breaking solidarity with our fellow parents. But if we have a real relationship with the parents and a real relationship with the child, and care about them both, there may be no greater act of respect or caring.

2

Cultivating Resilience

Bear the burden of one another's feelings; share the buoyancy of one another's strengths.

Range of motion

I was asking the doctor how to handle tendonitis. Should I extend my arm all the way even if it hurts, or should I be protecting it from strain as it heals? Her response was clear. Avoid sudden, sharp movements. Consider ice and anti-inflammatories for the swelling. But keep your full range of motion even if it hurts. Limiting range of motion will cause problems down the road. Her absolute certainty that full range of motion was the healthier choice helped me think about my arm. More important, it resounded in my head as a vast metaphor for life.

For so many of us, growing up is a gradual process of giving up our natural range of motion so as to avoid the pain that extending fully might cause. It certainly was for me. I learned to not show anger (and later, to not even notice feeling it), because anger was too painful for my parents to handle. I learned to not expect more than I was sure to be able to get, because expectation can lead to disappointment, for which there was no space. I learned to hold back around others unless I was completely confident, because risk was scary, humiliation lurked, and fear was a very painful emotion. I learned to do well at the things I was good at, and pretend I wasn't interested in the ones where failure was a possibility.

None of this has kept me from leading a life that is very good in many ways. Just as I can reach something by moving my whole body rather than extending my arm fully, I learned to compensate and manage pretty well. But that limited range of motion has definitely caused trouble—just as the doctor said it would. Fear of anger, reluctance to risk wanting things, and hesitance to put myself forward or show myself as a beginner have created a steady drag as I've worked to make a place for myself in this world.

The solution, however, is there. Just follow the doctor's orders and it's clear what to do: extend your arm all the way even if it hurts. The pain is just pain. It's not creating a further difficulty in itself. Limiting your range of motion in order to avoid the pain is the real problem. So the direction for my life is clear: extend. Risk wanting, welcome anger, put myself forward despite lurking humiliation—know that it may feel very painful and that's okay. Of course it will hurt to stretch where emotional muscles have been protected for years. Feeling the pain is not the problem; it's part of the solution.

Ultimately, inevitably, the metaphor speaks to me as a parent. What can I do to help my children retain—and regain—*their* full range of motion? How does my impulse to protect them from hard feelings actually contribute to loss of range of motion? It's good to notice that we have power here. If our children have learned to limit themselves in order to avoid feeling a pain that there is no space for, we can create that space. We can welcome the feelings that are ready to pour out—the disappointments, the fears, the anger. We can think about where they've lost range of motion and we can encourage them to stretch in those areas, letting them know that we know how much it might hurt, and being there to help them with the pain.

My mind is still spinning. Every time I stretch my arm, that wonderful complete extension (even with the pain that's still hanging around it) reminds me of the full range of motion that we all want and deserve in our lives.

Power and kindness

It was one of those warm January afternoons. My two children and two of their friends had convinced me to play "Cookie Monster" out on the sidewalk. I don't know where the game came from, but they've played it all their lives, and it's a favorite when adults are available. As the Cookie Monster (the adult role; I've never seen it given to another child), I chased the children (the cookies), following rules that are set up so that the adults can't win. With their bases strategically located on all the porch steps, they were hard to catch. If I did happen to get one, I got to pick the cookie up, gloating, and put it in the oven under a tree—after which I'd be able to eat it. But I always had to close my eyes and take a nap while it was cooking—that was one of the rules—and inevitably another cookie would save it from the oven while I was sleeping. Their running, cheering and laughing would wake me up—and I would see that I had lost once again.

After playing the game for a while, my youngest decided that it would be fun to be caught. So he'd take little pretend running steps without moving forward. I'd obligingly scoop him up and pop him in the oven—and he delighted in the whole process, knowing beyond a shadow of a doubt that he'd have all the fun of being rescued by other cookies while I took my nap. We played for a long time, and while being a constant loser is not my first idea of fun, I did get plenty of exercise—and they laughed and laughed.

A couple of days later, the three of us were playing War. I've never liked cut-throat competitive card games. But if small children want to play with "real" cards, War is a good one to start with since the rules are simple and absolutely no skill or strategy is required. (And, says the educator in me, they *do* get practice with numbers.) As we played, I was a little reassured to be the one who was losing decisively. Though they seemed to be accepting the gain or loss of cards with remarkable equanimity, I thought things would go better, and they'd enjoy it more, if they were winning.

When I noticed my eldest picking through his cards to choose what to play, I assumed he was trying to cheat. I was amazed to see him play those cards not to win, but to lose. I asked what he was doing and he said that my pile had gotten too low. He wanted me to have more cards! The younger one then noticed the imbalance and both began turning their winnings over to me for a while in order to even things out. I was dumbstruck. Who ever heard of kindness in a game of War?

And what a switch from Cookie Monster! Yet I think the two are related. The children had all the power in the Cookie Monster game; the rules were in their favor—a delicious contrast to normal adult/child relationships. Moreover, they were in total control of how much risk they wanted to take, how far from base to venture, knowing that they would triumph in the end. They came to War with the knowledge that they could beat an adult any time they played Cookie Monster—and have a great time together doing it. Power was not a scarce commodity. Winning was not an activity that set them in uneasy competition with their peers. They could afford to be kind.

Playfully pushing through fears

We were on a field trip, and when it came time to head into the woods, one little five-year-old balked. The others had gone on ahead, so I stayed back to try to figure this one out. "Why don't you want to go into the woods?" I asked. He responded that once in the woods he'd gotten a pricker in his thumb and it had hurt, though now it was out. What to do? It seemed a pity to let a little pricker from the past keep him from this adventure, yet I knew that this child was not easily moved once he'd taken a stand.

I've come up against children's fears plenty of times. I'm pretty good with the ones that seem substantial to me—high insecure places, big rooms full of strangers, fire. But it's hard when what they're afraid of seems so silly. They don't want to walk in the grass because they might step on a mole hill. They don't want to go on the sand because there might be a crab. They don't want to get in the water above their ankles for reasons they cannot articulate.

I don't feel very helpful at these moments. I want to give up in despair, ridicule them for the idiocy of their fears, force them into this objectively safe activity, or abandon them to stew in their stupid choices while I get on with enjoying my own life. I want to scream, "I can't believe it!"

Unfortunately, nothing that I want to do works. I've never seen a child get over such a fear through ridicule, domination, abandonment, or adult despair. The only thing I've found to be helpful is to offer myself as a safe resource, encourage them to pay attention to the scary thing, and let the fear show itself, with no worry when (if ever) they will get unscared enough to do what they couldn't do before.

I didn't know this child well, and wasn't sure if I could offer enough safety that he could use me as a resource. But I figured it was worth a try. So I said, "How about if I hold your hand and take responsibility for keeping the prickers away?" He wasn't sure. I said how much I wanted to try and how careful I would be. He finally agreed and took my hand to give it a try. (This in itself was a step forward in my relationship with this very self-contained, non-demonstrative child.)

I took the attitude toward the prickers that has worked well with my children in other situations: loud and menacing. "You'd better watch out prickers, because HERE WE COME! If you don't get out of our way, you're gonna be sorry, 'cause we're gonna STOMP on you." With this tone, the situation is turned upside down. WE are the all-powerful ones now, and it's the prickers that get to shake in their shoes.

He was clearly intrigued by this novel approach. But I wasn't able to protect him from one little prick, and he said he wanted to go back. I didn't try to push him, but continued to menace and stomp enthusiastically as we retraced our steps. Just as we were almost out of the woods, he changed his mind again. There was something about this adventure that he wanted more of. So we headed back in. While I threatened and subdued the big prickers, I pointed out little ones that he could stomp, and he got more and more daring as we went along. When we came to an open patch, he let go of my hand and ran on ahead. I maintained the tone, saying, "Phooey, no prickers here! Well, if there are any up ahead, they'd better just watch out!"

He had a good time at our destination and when we were ready to head back he took my hand and announced with pleasure that it was time to stomp more prickers. Another little girl perked up her ears at this tone, and the three of us threatened and stomped all the way back. He was still cautious for sure, but very much engaged in this daring adventure of facing the fear.

When his mother came to pick him up, he couldn't wait to tell the highlight of the field trip: "Mom, Pamela and I did a lot of pricker stomping!" And the next time I saw him, a week later, the first words out of his mouth were, "When are we going to have a chance to stomp some more prickers?" This was a fear that would never be the same again. And I was touched. With just a little initiative and thought on my part, I had reached a boy who seemed unusually reserved and inaccessible—and won his heart.

Catching the moment

We were unloading the car after a shopping trip, and the boys got in a fight about who was going to carry what. The younger one wanted the bag with the toys. The older one already had it. I suggested that they switch halfway to the house. At the switching point the younger one got the bag, but some overflow from it ended up in his brother's hands. He was complaining about the injustice of it when we reached the steps, but I was out of fresh ideas at that point and anyhow, the deed was done. I couldn't fathom why he was so upset by a few yards of sidewalk and a plastic bag.

But I had a little time and his brother was immediately and totally engrossed in the new toy. So I took him in my lap, commenting that I noticed how upset he was about the bag — and he burst into tears.

It's always easier for me to listen to a child crying than a child complaining. At least it feels as if *something* useful is happening. Even if I don't understand exactly what's going on, I have this image of pressure being released, of pus being drained away from a wound. It feels healthy.

So he cried and I kept talking to him, trying to get closer to what was really hurting. I called to mind everything I knew about him, and used the intensity of his tears to gauge my accuracy. (It's like that children's game of guiding someone to a hidden object by telling them how cold or hot they are: "You're freezing cold... you're getting warmer... colder... warmer again... *warmer*... HOT!")

"You wanted to carry the bag and the toy?" (tears). "It feels like things just don't go your way?" (more tears). "It feels like your big brother gets what he wants and you don't?" (big nods and tears). "It feels like he's first? Like we put him first?" (convulsive sobs).

HOT! Here is the center of the hurt. I'm taken aback, and very sorry that this wonderful child feels that way, even for a minute. Yet I'm sure that this is the right thing for us at this moment. I hold him close and he cries and cries. He doesn't say a word, so I keep up both ends of the conversation. I talk about his part, about how hard it is to be the younger child, and my part, of how wonderful he is and how sorry I am he feels that way, and how much I love him.

Then he's done. Just as with a scraped knee, after a while the pain goes away. He's ready to check out this new purchase, and moves easily into play with his big brother.

Nobody is to blame, nothing must be corrected, nothing more needs to be said. Lessons. Lessons. I'm always learning—and relearning—lessons. Things that seem little aren't little. Tears can heal. A wonderful opportunity may be at wait behind any free moment when we can choose to really pay attention.

Giving up versus wanting

One of the most exasperating qualities about young children is that they don't give up. They don't give up the toys they want when other children want them too. They don't give up the ideas that they have when those ideas are simply not workable. They are not easily distracted or satisfied by alternatives, even ones that would seem to have comparable value. They just know what they want, and keep wanting it—loudly, insistently, passionately.

It drives us crazy. Many parents focus an incredible amount of energy during these years on trying to "tone down" or "civilize" that wanting. We have a lot of adult ideas about how you're *supposed* to behave in these situations. You're *supposed* to share. You're *supposed* to think of the other person. You're *supposed* to compromise. You're *supposed* to take failure to get what you want quietly, and with good grace.

Yet there are several flaws in this approach. Sometimes we are righteously expecting our two-year-olds to do things that we are poor models of ourselves. (How good are we at sharing the things we are attached to—the TV during the football game, our money, our private stash of treasured make-up or fishing lures, or whatever?) Other times we have indeed learned, and do model these qualities, but at a greater cost than we would want any child to incur. (I, for one, am a great compromiser—so good that I have incredible difficulty even knowing what I want, much less holding out for it.) And requiring small children to stuff their feelings—not only to not get what they want, but to not show that they care—is just a recipe for trouble. Either you fail abysmally and everybody is mad, or you succeed beyond your expectations and get a child whose emotional life goes all the way underground.

This has not been an easy area for me. All my inclination and training set me up to expect children's pleasant cooperation with my benign authority, along with unceasing awareness of the needs and desires of others. But the qualities of passion and determination in children have grown on me steadily over the years.

When push comes to shove, I would rather have a child who is good at wanting than a child who is good at giving up. I would rather have a child who cries for his mom when she leaves than one who doesn't even notice or seem to care. I would rather encourage two little ones to want the same toy loudly and passionately at the same time, with no rush to a tidy solution, than to immediately cut off that process with an edict from above that they take turns. They won't always get what they want, but at least they get to want it.

I don't think children who are allowed this space will grow up rigid and selfish or totally uncontrolled. They still seem to learn about flexibility, real limits, and the legitimate needs of others. In the longer term they may learn it better than those who are hemmed in by moral requirements to do so. Perhaps even more important, we get to learn. Watching our children, we get to learn again about wanting, and passion, and not giving up on ourselves or the things we hold dear.

3

Cultivating Humility

Let us teach by being ourselves teachable.

I can't believe

"I can't believe he did that!" How often do we say this about our children? "I can't believe she stepped right in that mud puddle." "I can't believe he won't even try the slide." "I can't believe she would be so upset about such a little thing." "I can't believe they enjoy playing that game."

It's certainly a common refrain in my parenting, and the dominant emotion is usually despair: this child is acting in ways that make absolutely no sense to me, and I am at a total loss as to how to respond.

I was talking with a friend about one of these incidents, and found myself hearing the literal meaning of those words. "I can't believe he did that." How can I not believe something that I have been witness to? Surely, disbelieving a truth about a person can't put me on very solid ground in relation to them.

I'd been focused on how baffling I found *his behavior*. But it occurred to me, in this conversation, that the place to start might better be *my own disbelief*. What if I tried going with the truth of what I've witnessed instead? "This *did* happen, and it's important that I believe it."

From that perspective everything looks different. Somehow the disbelief had insulated me from the reality of the situation. After all, if someone does something that's beyond belief, then I'm absolved from the responsibility of handling it. I'm justified in my feeling that it's out of my control, hopeless, impossible, whatever.

Saying that I *do* believe it feels like a first step toward reclaiming my power in the situation. If I acknowledge that reality, then I can start *thinking* about it. If he really did do it, then something must have caused him to do it. If I have a hard time believing it, then there must be something that's giving me a hard time.

This new framework doesn't automatically provide answers. But at least it faces me in the right direction with the right questions in mind. I might not want to know about it. I might not want to acknowledge that he is that upset, or that angry, or that scared, or that different from me. But at least I'm dealing with what is. I'm on solid ground. Now I can take the next step: "Since this really is true, then it will be useful if I..." And, from the completion of that thought, a further step is likely to emerge.

After I'd started writing this, I was telling someone about an awkward little encounter and heard myself saying, "I can't believe I did that." (This time, the dominant emotion was shame.) What a gift to have this framework to fall back on: "You did do it, there was some reason, and there's a next step you can take." Thank goodness for what I learn as a parent!

Whose problem?

How often do we adults do what's necessary to stop a child's intolerable behavior, and congratulate ourselves on restoring a rational order to the environment, without ever considering what makes that behavior intolerable? By definition, it has to be behavior that the adult can't tolerate. Seen this way, the situation is not so clear. Is the problem the child's behavior or the adult's lack of tolerance?

While some behavior, like that which damages another person or the environment, can be objectively defined as needing to change, much of what we don't like lies in a great marshland of gray. Sometimes we can help problem solve and offer alternative ways of doing things, or help children drain the feelings that are contributing to that behavior. But other times, our feelings are part of the tangle. The only thing that's clear is that I don't like what's going on, and I want it to stop.

Then there are questions to ask myself (though, in reality, I don't usually think of them until later, after I've already intervened in some heavy-handed, adult-authority-wielding way). "Does this *always* bother me, or is it just getting me now?" "Does this bother *everybody*, or is it just me?" "Does this bother me when *every* child does it, or is it just this particular child?" "What is it that I simply can't stand?"

What I *can* do now, if I have a role, is to start talking with the children about the real source of the difficulty. I, for example, do most of my yelling when I'm particularly tired. Behavior that was perfectly acceptable from them yesterday—or fifteen minutes ago—now turns me into a screaming meanie. I've just run out of slack. And it's not that hard to let them know the story. "Boy, I'm really tired, you guys. I bet you can tell from the way I'm sounding."

They now have the information. They're not bad. They may have to take the brunt of my feelings for a while, but it's clear to all of us that they're not the cause of them. It's not ideal, but if I can be that clear (and so long as I don't damage them physically), we can make it through. Children actually seem quite responsive to this approach. After all, they have to find their way around the irrationalities of adults, often put forth as rules of behavior, all the time. It's probably very refreshing to have the reality acknowledged: we have our problems too.

I have a vivid memory of a time when I was at the end of my rope. Everything the children did or said was a new outrage, and I just couldn't stop yelling. Finally, my four-year-old took the toddler aside, explaining kindly to him: "Mommy's tired. She's going to yell. Let's go play." His voice was entirely free of either blame or shame. What a great gift to an overstretched mother—and what a hopeful sign for the future.

Love of learning

I had come to pick my son up at a friend's house. They had been berry-picking and the fruits of their labor were going into a shortcake. The other children had lost interest in the process and gone off to play, but my son was still in the kitchen. For some reason I saw him clearly at that moment. He was standing beside my friend as she stirred — watching with total absorption. His face was alight with the fullness of the moment. Clearly there was nowhere he'd rather be, nothing he'd rather be doing. This was love of learning in the purest form I've ever seen.

We all know that love of learning is a Good Thing. We want it for our children, and may suspect that to experience it in school is the exception rather than the rule. We probably encourage it unconsciously at home when we model our own love of learning (and probably discourage it unconsciously at other times). The question that was framed for me, in this picture of my son, was what to do when they love something that I don't.

It's no secret that I don't like to cook. I'm competent and efficient, but it's just work. My husband pointed out to me years ago that our son was interested in cooking. I couldn't imagine why, and it still remains hard to believe. On the rare occasions that I've remembered to invite him to work with me on dinner, his response has been lukewarm, and I've been just as glad to do it myself. My husband, who genuinely enjoys cooking, has had some good companionable times with him in the kitchen, but he's usually in a rush. Trying to be good parents, we've let him experiment with original baking recipes, trying to teach him what combinations will make the results palatable. But I've known that, somehow, none of this had really done him justice.

Watching him on this afternoon, however, it all began to fall into place for me. I'd had the part about learning, but not the part about love. Of course he doesn't choose to be in the kitchen with me. Who would want to learn drudgery? All of a sudden, I saw why the cooking shows on public TV attract him. These are people who love to cook. The solution isn't to try to instruct him better, or even find someone else to instruct him. The thing to do is to get him around people who love what he loves.

This might mean paying someone, but it might not. I talked with my friend about having him over to cook with her more often (at eight, he can be a real help now), and she was delighted. Who wouldn't want to share their valued store of knowledge with someone who is eager to learn it?

The lesson for me is that, as our children try to learn the things that are important to them, they are looking for more than facts, more than instruction. They are looking for a context in which the love, the excitement, the curiosity that they feel can be taken in and reflected back to them. They are looking for people who love what they want to learn, and love them for wanting it.

As I think about love of learning this way, I am challenged — both to match my children up more thoughtfully with the older people around them, and to be more open about what I love.

The taste of humiliation

We had arrived at my son's first gymnastics class. When I'd finally realized how passionately he wanted to take gymnastics, I'd put time and thought into finding the best situation that I could, and here we were. He was excited and ready to go. With his wonderful little body and his eagerness to adventure and use it in different ways, I was looking forward with pleasure to seeing him in this new milieu.

I was absolutely unprepared for what I saw. Compared with the other children in the group, he was totally uncoordinated and incompetent. He couldn't do some of the simplest things. His lack of ability stood out like a sore thumb, and it was painful to watch.

A good part of my attention during that hour went to thinking about what to say to him at the end. I could point out how he was the youngest, how some of them had taken the class before, how quickly he was probably going to improve. I could mention all the things that he *was* good at, to take some of the sting out of this experience. Would I be able to do a good enough job to prop up his self-esteem until the time came (and I fervently hoped it would be soon) when he could hold up his own in the group?

At the end of the class, maybe it was the undevastated look on his face that warned me. In any case, I set aside all my well-prepared reassurances for the moment and simply asked him how it had gone. "Great!" he said. What?! Totally taken aback, I asked him to say more. He told me the parts that were the most fun, how hard it was to figure out the cartwheels, what the teachers did, what he was best at.

I waited for more, but he was done. He had nothing to say about how terrible it feels to be incompetent, nothing about the humiliation of being the worst in the group, nothing about the pain of making mistakes in public.

I went home puzzling over the whole thing. Somewhere in that picture there *had* to be humiliation. I could feel it in my bones, taste it in my mouth. Why wasn't he showing any signs? It took me a while to realize that this was *my* humiliation. It's certainly a feeling that I've known well and tried my very best to avoid. I remembered what it was like having to step up to bat in junior high gym class, *knowing* that I would strike out, and standing there in front of everyone as the inevitable happened. I thought of how hard I always tried to appear competent, of what pains I took to protect myself from the possibility of making public mistakes or showing myself up as a clumsy beginner.

If *I* had been out on that gym floor displaying that level of beginnership, *I* would have felt like dying of mortification. *I* would have needed all those reassurances and more to be able to imagine facing that group again the following week. My son, however, is a different person, and had a totally different experience.

It's so easy to assume that anyone, and our children in particular, will feel the way we do that we may not notice when they are having quite a different experience. If their reactions do seem just the same, it's probably because we've trained them well in our own (less than completely confident and relaxed) point of view on the world. And I guess that's the one part of this incident I can claim with pride: I stopped myself from letting him know that he was supposed to feel humiliated. By keeping my hurt-laden point of view out of it, he was free to have his own, *much* healthier, reaction.

The question with no right answer

As a child, I remember learning the classic no-right-answer question: "When did you stop beating your wife?" We found it a clever and amusing trick. Someone had figured out a way to ask a seemingly innocent question that gave no option of an innocent answer.

It was the cleverness that stuck in my mind. But having the experience of being on the receiving end of that question, if only in my head, is something else entirely. "Why don't you *want* to act lovingly toward me?" I feel trapped by a question that labels me guilty regardless of the answer.

I wonder how much we do this to our children. We are mystified by their behavior, their seeming lack of desire to act like decent caring human beings. "Why don't you want to cooperate?" "Why do you enjoy being bad?" And the more we ask those questions, the more stubbornly they cling to behaviors and attitudes that seem totally inexplicable.

Something about being asked a question that assumes guilt leaves a person with little in the way of flexible response. The possibility that I actually *do* want to cooperate, *do* want to express love, *do* want to show my natural goodness, has been eliminated. My basic lack of common decency in this area is a given; the questioner just wants to know why.

What can I say? There is no defense. At the moment I'm asked, I'm likely to be feeling bad. I *don't* feel loving, I *don't* feel cooperative. I *don't* feel like being good. So the questioner's assumptions ring true. Maybe I really am a bad person—but I have no idea why. And if I'm being called a bad person and can say nothing to disprove it, then it's easier to act that way than to fight it. The question has helped lock me into the behavior that it was trying to challenge.

What if we took a totally different tack? What if we assumed that our children—or anybody else in our lives for that matter—are completely good, regardless of what they do. The question of a non-cooperative child shifts from "Why are you bad?" to "What is making you, a basically cooperative human being, act this way?" The question of one who is withholding affection becomes, "What's happened that is obscuring your loving nature?" The question of a child whose behavior is outrageous becomes, "Why are you, who are so good, doing these things?"

The answers may not come fluently and smoothly. They may not be easy to hear. But at least they are there. "I'm mad." "I haven't been heard and am looking for a way to show." "I'm hurting." The ground may be rocky, but at least it is solid. Their basic goodness is not in question. An answer is possible.

4

Cultivating Connection

Live affectionately as friends, entering into the joys and sorrows of one another's daily lives.

Peek-a-boo

Peek-a-boo. How often have we played that game—with our own children, grandchildren, nephews and nieces, neighborhood children, babies that we don't even know at the check-out line at the grocery store or on the bus? It may be called different things in different places, but its theme is universal and eternal.

I must have played peek-a-boo a thousand times before I ever noticed what the game was really about. It happened at a workshop, when I had just met somebody new. We liked each other right away, found a topic of mutual interest without difficulty, and were chatting away happily. Then came a lull in the conversation—one of those pregnant pauses—when our eyes met, when we both had to notice that the other one was really there. How excruciatingly embarrassing! Luckily, we were both on the same wavelength, We looked, and laughed, and hid our faces, looked again, and laughed and laughed.

It was a classic game of peek-a-boo. And no wonder the game is a classic. It's all about the most basic questions in human relationships: Are you there? Are you really there? Will you be there next time? Do you see me? Do you really see me? Are you pleased to see me? Will you be pleased to see me next time? Not only do you get a chance to ask all those important questions. You get to laugh and laugh as the answers come back—a great and wonderful string of unqualified yeses.

Ultimately, peek-a-boo is a game about noticing, about being there. To be played successfully, both players must have their full attention on the game. This, I think, may be its greatest attraction. Any child who is playing peek-a-boo has secured another person's undivided positive attention—one of the most scarce and valuable resources of all. No wonder children love the game.

And no wonder we adults found it such an embarrassing game to play with each other. In the course of our childhood and growing up, we've gotten enough no's in response to all those questions that they often seem like pretty scary ones to ask. (I think of all the hundreds of times I've turned my children down: "No, other things are more important." "No, I don't have time for you." "No, I would rather not be bothered." "No, you'll have to manage by yourself.") It's not surprising that we've found lots of ways to avoid risking those no's. We don't ask. We go off by ourselves. We lower our eyes. We change the subject. We deflect with a joke. We discover important work that needs to be done.

But peek-a-boo is a great game. I have a new appreciation of why children want to play, and I'd like to see it played even more—with all sorts of variations for different ages. What if every child riding on a bus, every child waiting in a line got to play peek-a-boo? What if that were just the beginning? The more yeses we can get to those basic questions, and the more we can laugh in wonder and delight at all the yeses, the better off all of us will be.

Banking quality time

We know we are supposed to spend quality time with our children. But how do we find enough time if we work outside the home? How do we focus it if we're at home with multiple demands of multiple children? Most vexing of all, is the time that we find to spend good enough? Is it really quality time?

I remember being at a family weekend where parents were asked to pair up with children for an hour of "special" time. Our task was to be fully available to that child, to do exactly what they wanted us to do. What an opportunity! What a chance for that rare and highly prized quality time!

In the evening there was a question period. One woman asked plaintively, "What if you wasted your special time? My daughter didn't want to do anything special. So we spent the whole hour wandering around, looking at bushes and things. What use was that?"

I've never forgotten the answer she got. "Nothing special has to happen. Your daughter had your attention. She knew that she had it; she knew its value. If she didn't have any particular use to make of it right then (to talk about a trouble, share a confidence, master a skill), that's fine. Think of it as banking. That hour of attention has been banked. She's richer by that much resource. It's in her account now and will be available whenever she needs it."

I think this concept of banking can help take the mystique out of quality time. We don't have to go to some special event and be magically uplifted together. We don't have to have the parent-child conversation of a lifetime. We don't have to have the most exciting thrill of our lives. We don't have to create the situation that evokes the perfect feeling. Any of these are fine if they happen, but they're all a little hard to guarantee, and they aren't necessary for quality time. Pinning our hopes on them does little more than feed parental inadequacy and guilt—which will flourish just fine without additional help.

The key to quality time is our attention. And we can pay good attention to our children wherever we are, and whatever they are doing. It doesn't have to feel special to us. We can look through fashion magazines, arrange little cars or figures, go shopping, take a walk, joke around, paint a room, look at bushes, draw pictures, have water fights, listen to their complaints. It doesn't matter what we do together. It just matters that they make the choice and have our attention.

Of course, this is more easily said than done. My impulse to try to get some work done while pretending to pay attention is almost overwhelming at times, and the activity of their choice is not always the one I would prefer. But when we can actually be available to them, and pay good attention, whether for ten minutes or an hour, they will notice. It's a precious resource and they will use it — cashing in right away or enriching their account in the bank.

Independence and isolation

We took bikes down to the park on a beautiful Sunday afternoon, and I was surprised when my younger son wanted me to keep a hand on his back. He's been able to keep his balance for over a year, has ridden by himself many times, and is, in general, a very competent independent little person. Why would he want a mother's hand on his back when he could do it all by himself?

As I listened to my questions, I started hearing them in a different way. Why would someone ask for support when they didn't absolutely require it? Why would anyone choose human contact over independence? It got me wondering again about whether we push our children too fast, too relentlessly, toward independence? It seems that all our values are geared in that direction.

We take such pride in our children's independence. The baby can amuse herself. He can sleep through the night by himself. She can walk by herself. He can get to school by himself. True, there is a very natural urge on the part of a young person to master new skills, to become able to do things they couldn't do before. But I wonder how much we let this budding competence flower in its own good time, and how much we push for the earliest possible bloom.

Sometimes a child is clearly striving for mastery in some area and wants our help getting there. But how often do we push for independence as its own goal? This seems to be a particular issue for little boys. We're supposed to push them out, train them to go it alone.

The messages are pervasive, but I'm not convinced. It doesn't seem likely that a childhood of training for lonely independence will result in a fulfilled, happy life, rich in human contact. (I was certainly trained that way, and one of the greatest struggles of my adult life is finding my way back to real contact with other human beings.)

My guess is that we would do better to stay close as long as we can. This doesn't mean using them to meet some deep unmet need of our own—which can be very hard on children. Rather, it means offering lots of warm human contact, inviting them towards us rather than pushing them away.

It means holding our little babies—though we can probably never figure out how to do it as much as they would choose. It means keeping a lap available to our boys as well as our girls, as they grow older. (I remember how startled I was seeing a fifteen-year-old boy in his father's lap, then, recovering from the shock, recognizing a touching challenge to the assumption of teenage isolation.)

It means noticing when our children want us, remembering that sometimes a request for help is really a request for human contact. It means being willing to stay close to our six-year-old bikers sometimes, just for closeness' sake—even though we both know that they could do it all by themselves.

Being there

I always had the idea that there was a direct correlation between children growing older and the job of parenting getting easier.

Of course, there are ways in which this is true. My children are no longer totally dependent on me. Nor are they constantly calling for my attention or asking for my help. There are more and more things that they can do for themselves and on their own. (Some of this blessed independence, of course, is a little frightening, like exploration of the boundaries of the internet or the public transit system.)

But there are things that are actually harder. In the old days, when I had something I needed to do in the evening or on the weekend, I would just make a childcare arrangement, pack them off, and do what I needed to do. Now their wishes have to be part of the equation. They are old enough to know what they want to be doing and who they want to be doing it with. What's most convenient for me cannot always carry the day.

Or I find myself assuming that a parenting role will be required on a weekend when my husband is out of town, and limiting my personal planning so I can be available to the boys. Then they make their own arrangements to be with friends and I'm left hanging. For someone who's trying to take this job of parenting seriously, I can end up feeling pretty inconsequential and useless.

But then there are the times when my oldest comes home from school and asks if I'm going to be around for the whole evening. His clear satisfaction in hearing that I am gives me a clue. It's not that he wants my attention or my company all evening. He definitely doesn't. He just wants to know that I'm going to be available if he should need me.

I think this is my lesson for this stage of parenting. I am no longer indispensable for the tasks of daily survival. But they still want me there. And if I can remember that just being there is important, I get some wonderful gifts.

My oldest, for example, rarely answers questions about his day or his thoughts or his hopes with more than a monosyllable. But if I stop asking, and just hang out—in the car, at the kitchen table, over late-night weekend TV—he starts volunteering information. I get to hear the funny stories from school, the new plan around saving and spending money, thoughts about friends, the latest science fiction or invention concept.

Paradoxically, the less I seem invested in good communication while hanging out, the more I get. I remember coming home from a long Saturday of physical labor and plopping down on the couch, not interested in doing anything myself, not even able to care about what he should be doing. He found this total lack of agenda on my part very attractive, and settled right in for some good joking and chatting and general quality time.

Being there in this way for our older children certainly doesn't seem as vital as spooning baby food or helping with shoes or reading aloud. It's less immediately gratifying than snuggling at bedtime or tending to a boo-boo. But they are counting on us for it.

Abuse and protection

A young adult was talking about what it was like to have experienced sexual abuse as a child. It became very clear in the telling that, while the experience itself was painful, what followed when it was over was even worse. Still just a little boy, he had to face living with it for the rest of his life. With no one to tell, no way to get perspective on why it had happened, on who was to blame, he had to carry it with him, as part of his definition of himself. I was appalled. The incident itself, terrible as it was, paled in comparison with the lonely pain of making it part of his life.

What a difference it would have made if he could have told! The picture is so clear in my mind. A loving mother or father would have gathered him into their arms, and—maybe slowly at first—the whole experience would all have come pouring out. He would have gotten absolute reassurance that no part of it was his fault. He would have soaked up their confidence that he was absolutely good, that he had never deserved this, that they would do their absolute best to ensure that it would never happen again. He would be left with a memory of a painful, ugly experience—and nothing more.

I thought of this young man later at our parent and toddler

group. One mom was worrying about how to protect her child, whose sunny outgoing disposition made her attractive to all the adults around. Was it safe for her daughter to be that friendly? Should she start teaching about danger, telling her child never to talk to strangers? What a pity that would be—training her to mistrust other human beings. But was there a responsible alternative?

The sad thing here is that we can never fully protect our children from bad things happening. Adults have the power to take advantage of even the most mistrustful child, and the never-talk-to-strangers rule can't shield children from the majority of abuse, which comes from people they know and have some reason to trust.

But we're far from powerless here. We can talk with them about not going off with strangers. We can remind them that they get to choose about how they are touched. Most of all, we can protect our children from the deep and corrosive on-going hurt of living alone with an experience of abuse. We can make sure that they know, beyond a shadow of a doubt, that they can tell us *anything*, no matter what.

Of course, it's not as easy as it sounds. When one of the issues is sex, how many of us are ready to have open, relaxed discussions about it with our children? And there are lots of times when inviting them to tell us what's really going on is the last thing we want. Who gets excited about the prospect of hearing one more complaint, one more disappointment, one more problem, one more upset, from one more little child? Who really wants to know all the details of teenage angst? Our overstretched lives would seem much easier if they would just button up and do what needs to be done. And when what we want most of all is for our children to be happy, it's hard to invite and coax out their feelings of fear and grief.

But this is their greatest protection. If they know that it's safe to tell anything, that we want to know, that our arms and hearts are open to all their stories and all their feelings, then they have a way to heal, a way to move forward. Then any abusive incident can become simply that, an incident, and they are free to go on living their lives, secure that they are good, and loved, and not alone.

5

Cultivating Discernment

Attend to Pure Wisdom and be teachable.

Promises from our childhood

Long ago I made a sacred promise to myself that, when I had children, I would never subject them to what was hardest about my own childhood. I think many parents do this. It is part of the upward trend in the universe—each generation trying to make life better for our children. Every parent who makes such a promise deserves our complete appreciation, congratulations and support.

It's helpful to keep in mind at the same time, however, that we can keep getting smarter. We don't want to stick with the rigidity of an old promise if there's something even better to hold on to.

The big promise that I made to myself was to never hold my children responsible for meeting my emotional needs. I wouldn't bring children into this world to meet my personal needs for companionship, or a sense of future, or a way to feel useful. I would have them because it was a wonderful opportunity to nurture new life. I wouldn't require behavior of my children because it made *me* feel better. I would try to think through what behavior made sense, made *their* lives go well—and take my own emotional needs and difficulties to other adults.

It was a good promise. I think it's very easy to unconsciously burden our children with responsibility for our emotional well-being, and many of them try hard to carry that responsibility, at considerable cost to their own well-being.

I'm proud of the job I've done in this regard, but I'm beginning to realize that there has been a cost. In promising myself so faithfully to not require them to tend to my needs, there's a way that I've written myself out of the picture of family life. I encourage them to say what *they* want, and neglect to notice what *I* want. I ask them about *their* day and don't think to tell about *mine*. I invite them to share what's hard for *them,* but resolutely keep to myself what's hard for *me*. I do well by them in many ways, but much of the person that I am stays hidden behind the role.

It may be partly that I haven't kept pace with their growing up. What may have been appropriate for infants and toddlers is no longer necessary for ten- and thirteen-year-olds. Not only do I think it would be better for *me* to show more of myself, I think it would be better for *them*. They deserve to be living with a real live human being, not just someone inhabiting a mom suit.

That promise from my childhood was a good one. I'm glad I made it. But I don't think it can carry me or my family any further. It was a correction of an imbalance from my childhood, but now the balance has swung too far the other way. It's time to lay it down and make a new promise to myself. I don't know exactly what it will be, but I know it's there waiting to be found.

Many of us made promises about how we would be as parents, and I think they were always good. But I wonder how many of those promises—like mine—have become unwieldy and even problematic as time goes by. I'd like to offer museum space to old promises, where they can be treasured and respected and valued for the role they played, so we can lay them down and be free to make new promises for the present and the future.

Small human beings—stimulating company

"First my parents' friends make my little brother the center of attention, then they don't want to pay any attention to him. It's like they want to turn him on and off." I was struck by the acuteness of this older sibling's observation.

I think it's hard for all of us to figure out how to treat very small human beings. There is something so fresh and endearing about them that we are irresistibly attracted. Their unconscious pleasure and innocence are such a wonderful contrast to our worries, our inhibitions, our exhaustion, our preoccupations with what others will think. They give us a fresh glimpse of what life could really be like. They recharge us.

But then, there is the other side. They fuss. They cry. They call for attention when we have other plans for it. They call insistently. What they are interested in and challenged by has long since ceased to interest or challenge us.

These reactions to very small children seem opposite, but there is a common theme. The focus is on us, and how they make us feel. When we could use some charm and innocence and a reminder of the goodness of life, we find babies useful. When we have our own agendas, we can easily find them a nuisance. We do indeed want to turn them on or off.

The perspective that I'm finding most intriguing these days is that very small children are inherently interesting human beings. How they perceive the world is interesting. How they take on new challenges is interesting. How they figure out their relationships to others is interesting. If my goal when I am around small children is to notice, not how they make me feel, but what they are trying to do and how they are doing it, then they are invariably stimulating company.

It's taken a while. I can remember being consumed by impatience at my toddlers' pace and choice of activity. I have foggier memories of when they were babies and it didn't look as if they were doing *anything*. But I am glad to still have infants and toddlers in my life, because I see a challenge here now that I'm eager to take on.

When a small child wants a book read aloud six times in a row, the obvious adult reaction is to be bored. The more interesting one is to try to figure out what that child is trying to accomplish by the repetition. When a baby makes eye contact under certain conditions and not others, it may not look like much is happening. But something is clearly going on, and trying to solve the puzzle of *what* is a task worthy of all my adult experience, wisdom and observational skills.

I think the moral is simple. Human beings are just plain interesting—with age as a totally irrelevant factor. And those interactions we find the most interesting will be the ones in which we pay closest attention to the other person, really wanting to know who they are, separate from us, and what they are trying to do.

Age-appropriate expectations

We were at a weekend gathering of families, and I found myself seeing my seven-year-old in a new light. Either the context brought out fresh responses, or I had the leisure and awareness to observe things that usually go unnoticed. Whatever the reason, he kept slipping out of this tidy little pigeonhole that I'd made for him on the basis of his age, sex and dominant traits. He kept surprising me.

First, he made friends with a young woman in her early twenties—got to know her, found out things they both liked to do, and arranged time together—in a way that defies my conception of age-appropriate behavior (and she seemed to value this new friendship as much as he did). Then he chose to sit in on an adult discussion of parenting skills, and was clearly paying close attention. Finally, he was eager to take time out from play to be in a young people's support group. (I had calculated in advance who among those present might be interested, and discounted him automatically as too young.)

Clearly, I had underestimated this playful, adventurous little seven-year-old boy. On reflection, I think this is a pretty common trap for parents. Our fixed perceptions of what *should* be going on for our children can easily prevent us from seeing what actually *is*.

Although I went into parenting convinced that we often underestimate the intelligence and abilities of children, my expectations in that regard have been consistently too low. I remember babies understanding things way before I thought they would, a toddler thinking about my comfort before I could believe that capacity was developed, my eldest at four counseling his little brother (wisely) on how to deal with my anger. Even though they may not talk about it much, these small people know a *lot* about what's going on. I doubt if any amount of respect for their awareness can be too high.

On the other hand, our expectations of what they should be able to *do* at a certain age may easily be either too high or too low. All the emphasis on child development in our society carries with it a trap. We all know the months, or years, by which children are generally achieving milestones, and naturally we apply these guidelines to our children.

If they're early, we can bask in the knowledge that we have an "advanced" child. But if they're late, it's another story. We can easily be worried about their failure to perform "on schedule," and that worry can affect both them and our relationship to them. (I think of how incredibly difficult it was for me to come to terms with the fact that my eldest was still not a reader long after the age when I was reading with ease.) Yet children do have their own timetables, and it would be wonderful for them as well as us to be released from the tyranny of the norm.

So how do we keep our expectations high without falling into a trap? It can help if we think of our children not as slowly-evolving future adults, but as complete human beings in the present. Then we can notice what they actually do, invite them to new possibilities, relax, and appreciate them for the unique and wonderful people that they are right now.

Negotiating "cool"

My little boy never used to be cool. He used to snuggle up for bedtime stories, wrestle and laugh with me, want me close by. I never really thought about teenage years much. I guess part of me had the idea that *my* child wouldn't change. His voice dropped and he started to grow like a weed, and still he was my same sweet guy. This was going to be easy, I thought.

Then he got cool. All of a sudden snuggles were out. Hugs and kisses were deflected with bored disinterest. He didn't want my help with little things that I'd always helped him with before. My feelings were definitely hurt. Had I been totally written out of his life, virtually from one month to the next?

Thank goodness for friends who had already struggled through this stage. Left to myself, I would have taken all those messages at their face value, decided that he really didn't want me anymore, and quietly retreated, making no more moves in his direction, just hoping that someday he might change his mind and want me again.

But one friend in particular had taken on the mission of helping parents of teenagers. Her voice rang in my ears. "You get to be close forever. They still want you. They want to be close. They won't show it in the same way, but they're counting on you to not give up. You get to be close forever." The signs did not look promising, but I clung to the hope that she was right.

I decided to not give up. I made tentative little advances in his direction. Some were accepted with what looked like bored indifference. Some were deflected with more of the same. My feelings were hurt all over again. I cried with my husband. It would have been so much easier to stop trying—except that the price was losing my precious son even more finally.

And there was something about my friend's voice that rang true. "They're counting on you not to give up." I could imagine someone slipping into a suit of "cool" and seeing if they could fool their loved ones. "Hey, can you still recognize me in this outfit? Bet you can't!" In a way it was like a test. "Will you not get confused even if I try to confuse you?" "Will you remember who I really am underneath, even though I don't let any of that part show?" I don't quite understand the drive to play that game, but I sure know the right answer. (All of a sudden, I am reminded of our toddlers' transparently-simple games of hide and seek and peek-a-boo. "Even though I'm hidden, can you still find me!?")

There can be only one right answer. "Yes!" "Yes, I can find you." "Yes, you can count on me!" When I can remember all of that, I can remember to be more bold in showing my love — not putting out a tentative little feeler then dropping back and waiting for a totally positive response before making another move, but acting like someone who is confident of loving and being loved, and not worrying about what the response will be. It doesn't often look "sweet" these days. We're more likely to have laughing, funny-insult-trading, sparring matches than cozy snuggles. But when I boldly assume my welcome, he almost always responds. And to see his face open up in laughter as we play, to see that facade of "cool" drop away, if only for a moment, is all that I need to keep going. I still have my son.

Judgment and danger

One day at the zoo, my boys were clambering over one of the many little animal statues scattered enticingly around. Another child made a move to join in and his mother admonished him sharply. "Don't climb that! It's too dangerous!" I looked at the statue, at my children's enjoyment of that clearly-manageable but exciting physical challenge, and wondered about judgment and danger.

I remember being awed at the physical abilities of my children at a very early age. I tried to control my automatic assumption of danger as they explored. ("It's too high for you."

"That's not safe.") But I certainly stayed close, to notice what they could handle, and be able to respond if they couldn't. They rarely needed me.

My conclusion is that, if we give them a chance to explore from early on, they seem to develop remarkably accurate judgment about what they can and cannot handle. It can be scary for us. I remember when a mother brought her eighteen-month-old to our parent and toddler group, and the little girl headed straight for the big slide and began climbing up the rungs with great excitement. Her mother's response of "That's too high for you" came automatically, but the other teachers had seen children that age manage the slide fine, so they encouraged the mother to let her child try. Several adults, seeing the mother's fear, positioned themselves to protect the child from danger, and she climbed and slid and climbed and slid with great delight—and no need of assistance.

It was the mother who was having a hard time. She didn't like heights or slides. She was overwhelmed by the potential for danger and the urge to protect, and couldn't notice that her child was safe. Her judgment call, based on her own fears, simply didn't fit the situation.

We can't ignore the possibility of danger, or our role in protecting our children from it. But fear is nobody's friend. When you're afraid, you don't think well. Our goal, rather, is to give them the information, confidence and experience to manage situations that might otherwise be dangerous.

If we are always the ones to make judgment calls for our children, they may absorb our fears and limit what they try. While this may be convenient for us in the short run, they never learn what they can actually handle. Or they may react against our fears, heading repeatedly toward danger, a stance that can also bring trouble. Neither response leaves them flexibly capable of figuring out new things for themselves, based on their growing self-knowledge.

Children are eager to make their own judgments, to flex those muscles and taste that power. If we don't allow them enough space to judge for themselves, we'll have to deal with the power issue on different, and perhaps more difficult, terrain.

6

Cultivating Joy

Thus we are able to sense the Inward Light and to follow its leadings.

Can growing up be fun?

A friend mentioned casually one night that one of the most useful things we can do for our children is to show them how much we enjoy our own lives. "Think of what makes you happy," she said, "and figure out how to have more of that."

What a simple idea, yet how profound! Our children's main idea of what adulthood will look like for them is what they see in their parents' lives. Is that picture something to look forward to, or something to anticipate with dread?

What did my children see in my life, I wondered? Hard work, responsibility, a decent relationship with their father, respect for others, patience (sometimes), a willingness to be fair. Not a bad lot to look forward to, I thought, but certainly not real *attractive* or *fun*.

I started thinking about what makes me happy. Ice-skating on a frozen pond in winter—wonderful, but not something I can share with them very often. An undisturbed breakfast with the newspaper—a rare occurrence as well, and one that, by definition, can't happen when the children are around to see. Putting out a good piece of writing—but that, again, works best alone (it's in the middle of the night as I write this). Being of use to others, helping people untangle the threads of knotty situations and live their lives with more power—fine sounding words, but how do you share such a love with small children?

As I listened to myself consider and then discount each thing that came to mind, I began to wonder if maybe I was really a failure as a role model. Yet the problem seemed to lie more in the discounting. Nothing that made me happy, that voice said, could possibly be of any use to my children. What if I took the opposite position: anything that makes me happy is of great use to them, no matter how fleeting or profound. In that case my love of ice-skating, even if seen rarely, will be noticed, and *telling* them about it, as well as showing it, makes sense.

What if I told them every time I was happy (and there are usually such moments, even in the most humdrum or worst of days)? "I am having such a good time taking this walk with you." "I *love* the illustrations in this book." "Isn't the moon beautiful!" "It's so exciting seeing you learn to cook." Often I let those times go by unacknowledged, depriving both them and me of that chance to notice how full of good and rich moments my life is.

What about those loves that seem too adult, or happen when the children aren't there? What if I could start sharing those too? Some wouldn't be too hard: "I just read such a good letter from my sister." "I sure do love your Daddy." "I'm going to teach my class now because it's Monday night—and because I love it." "I'm so glad that we can have people from other countries staying in our house." Even as I write, horizons are starting to open. Why *not* notice how much I love life? Why *not* share it?

Why not try the ones that are even harder? "I'm really proud of the job I did helping a little girl in pre-school this morning." "I'm so pleased that a man I work with has come to trust me a lot." "I'm buying this for my friend in Uganda because she does such good work and I want to be a part of it." Why not? At worst the context would be missed and it would go over their heads. But they would surely get, and remember, the tone of pleasure in my voice. Or they might ask questions, and we would get a chance to talk about what I love.

In either case, *I* would get to notice—and that may be the key. If I can stop and notice what makes me happy, rather than just living each day as a series of obligations to be performed to the best of my ability, then they will surely start getting the idea that adulthood is another very good stage of life.

"Look, Mommy!"

I'd made an exciting fossil find and couldn't wait to show it to my husband, who had taken the by-then-bored children off to be amused. The picture was clear in my mind: I'd lay out the rocks and point. He would exclaim at some, and we would wonder together about the mysteries in others. It would be the perfect completion of the adventure.

Well, when we found each other, he was distracted and rushed. We had to eat before the place closed, and the children were full of news from their own adventure. My find got a brief, vague acknowledgment, and life moved on. I was amazed at how deeply disappointed and angry I felt in the face of this inattention. It made me wonder if I'd found treasure at all, or just a bunch of old rocks. The whole world looked gray.

It occurred to me that this response seemed a bit childish— which naturally got me thinking about children. How often our young children want us to notice their discoveries about themselves and the world. "Look what I found!" "Look what I made!" "Look what I can do!" They are so excited—and we have so little attention.

How can a bug on the sidewalk compete with a list of pressing errands, and what's that exciting about a bug anyway? How can the thirty-fifth jump off the couch or the thirty-sixth picture on the same theme be expected to attract fresh delight from an overworked parent?

Yet they do expect it. Not only that, they want it passionately, and it takes them a long time to give up. I think there's a lesson for us here. Our children are excited, and their excitement is real. What they perceive as a treasure is a real treasure to them. This openness to being truly excited, to finding treasure in unexpected places, is one of the great gifts of life that our children are ready—eager, bursting—to give us, over and over again. All we have to do is accept.

Of course it's easier said than done, but I think there's a lot in it for us. What if, by listening fully to words and tone of voice, we can catch a glimpse of the wonder of a bug—or any other miracle of life? What if, by watching the thirty-fifth jump with real interest, we get to see the exuberant vitality that is the birthright of every human being? What if, by asking about the thirty-sixth picture with our full attention, we can be reminded about our child's unique creativity and the creativity of all of us?

The more we can do this, the more we'll be helping our children hang on to their excitement about life, a wonderful quality that is so often lost too early. At the same time, we'll be holding up a model for sharing our own excitements, undeterred by the distracted, rushed or jaded grown-ups around us.

The pleasures of homework

It was Saturday afternoon. My son wanted help with his poetry homework. Having gotten an extremely attractive offer for an overnight adventure that would last through mid-afternoon on Sunday, he knew he had to get started if he wanted to go.

So far as I can tell, there is nothing that interests him about this poetry work. I can't say that I blame him. Reading "good literature" and answering textbook questions about it has never been my idea of fun. But I was delighted that he was showing so much initiative (liberating me from the role of nag) and was very willing to help.

The delight, however, was short-lived. He simply *would not take the job seriously*. After reading the poem aloud, I said, "Okay, the first question they ask is 'Why might the poet have chosen this topic?'" He considers with pleasure. "I know! He was being paid!" When I don't sound enthusiastic about that being the thing to write down, he starts guessing wildly—with even greater pleasure. "His brain was missing? Someone was threatening him with a gun? He was dead? They *all* were dead? Hey, I have a great idea, Mom! For every answer, I'll write, 'He did it because he was being paid.'" Now this is a pretty original, funny response. But it doesn't get him closer to completion, and it certainly doesn't make me feel like much help.

Luckily we're both pretty relaxed and in good communication with each other, and the time situation is not yet desperate—Sunday bedtime is still a long ways off—so there's a little slack. The strategy I choose is to beat on him (lightly, affectionately) for being so "wrong" while continuing to try to move the process along. We make some progress, though he continues to up the ante, make more jokes, take it less seriously.

He's having a great time, hanging out with his mom, making some progress on his homework, having fun. I, on the other hand, feel incredibly torn. I'm unwilling to bring down the heavy hand of authority, make it clear beyond a shadow of a doubt that this is *not* fun, *not* creative, *not* interesting, but *a job that has to be done and done right*. After all, I spent my whole school career with exactly that attitude and I wouldn't wish it on anybody else. But I'm going crazy with his tone of total irreverence, total unconcern with the product. I can't play the heavy with any enthusiasm, but I can't give up totally on the parental role and just join the fun.

Finally, I can no longer play the middle road—rolling with the jokes and relaxedly moving the process along. I up the ante myself. Rather than just beating on him, I grab him by the shirt front and start mock-yelling: "I can't stand this anymore. You're not doing it the right way. This is *work*. You're supposed to give the right answers and not joke around. I know what I'm talking about. I did this for thirteen years. So what if it's no fun—there's a right way to do it, and *this is not it*. You're driving me crazy!"

He smiles at me and says warmly and simply, "I know."

This totally unexpected response leaves me with a pretty big question: Who is doing the helping here? And who is doing the learning? True, I help him put down the "right" answers to poetry comprehension questions and keep him company in the homework process. But he requires me to examine what is really important, and welcomes my outbursts as I struggle. I hope he comes out ahead. I certainly do.

Love of work

My five-year-old was helping me disassemble some steel shelving. I held the nut with pliers while he worked on the bolt with a screwdriver. Eight nuts and bolts to a shelf. Four shelves. He worked hard; his tongue stuck out in concentration. He had to keep shifting his chair to get the best leverage, remembering which way to turn the screwdriver, and moving the container that held the loose nuts and bolts to keep it at hand. He was totally absorbed. It was clear that he had claimed this work as his own.

As I held the pliers, and shifted the ever-loosening shelves to ease the strain on the bolts, I thought about work. It was not easy to stand there, pliers in hand, and watch him struggle so laboriously with each nut. I could have done the job in far less time by myself. I kept trying to find ways to speed the process along, without taking it over. But all the while, I was aware of what a privilege it was to be with someone who showed such respect and love for work.

I've seen it in a lot of children, especially toddlers. They have discovered that they have enough skill, coordination and mobility to do things. They can hold a broom. They can carry clothes. They can dip a plate in and out of soap suds. What an accomplishment! What a joy to be able to participate so fully and responsibly in the life of the family!

My guess is that this love of work is part of every child's birthright. We want to gain skills. We want to play a role in shaping our world. We want to be of use. Yet by the time many children are six or seven, or eleven or twelve, things have changed. Work is a burden, an externally imposed drudgery, something to be gotten over with quickly, or avoided if possible. Some of us, as adults, have found work that we love. But for many of us, work is just a job to be gotten through, a necessary evil, a means to other ends.

I wonder what we can do as parents to help our children hold on to that early love of work. I remember the mixed feelings I had when my children were little. A toddler with a broom or on a chair at the sink is certainly an endearing sight. But I would inevitably be left with even more work, cleaning up after all their help. I was glad when I could remember that their pleasure in the work and the opportunity to be of use was worth a little of my time.

Once they are older, and we count on them to help out, it's even trickier. It's then that we start sending them clear messages that work is a drag. "You have to clean up. I don't care if you don't like it. Somebody has to do the work and there's no way I'm going to let you wriggle out of it." Maybe the solution is two-pronged: to make the repetitive work that nobody seems to like as much fun and soon over as possible, and to remember to talk about and include them as much as we can in the work that we love.

Watching my son as I worked with him on the shelving was a gift in my life. Making the effort to help keep that love of work alive in him is an investment whose returns could be of great value to both of us.

Leaning on each other

Another parent and I were on our way back to the car after an outdoor adventure with the children (then ages five, four, four and two), when they discovered a big, deep and irresistibly inviting mud puddle. (I had noticed it on the way out, and had carefully not called attention to it, casually steering them in a slightly different direction.) Having found it, they couldn't resist trying it out just a little bit—and immediately checked us out to see what our response was going to be. Now I try to be relaxed about things like water and dirt, guessing that the pleasure they give the children probably outweighs my desire for cleanliness and order, and I knew that this other dad felt the same. But this was a very big and very muddy puddle.

I looked at him and he looked at me. If I had been alone, I know I would have hustled the children away from all that dirt and water and gotten them safely into the car as soon as possible. If he had been alone, he probably would have done the same.

But we had each other. Taking a middle course, we suggested that they wade a little, but try not to get very wet. This invitation to restraint, however, was doomed from the start (as I think we had both secretly known it would be). Small children, faced with a big puddle and given a little permission, are not likely to exercise moderation. They were in up to their ankles, then the tops of their boots, then above. Once it had gotten that far, there was no logical limit. Soon they were up to their knees. Then, inevitably, one of them fell all the way in. He squealed with pure pleasure and invited the others to join him. They raced and slid and splashed and fell—and howled with delight. My friend and I kept looking at each other as the children got wetter and muddier and happier, both of us counting on the other's support to get us through.

Finally, we came to an ending place. (I don't remember clearly, but I think it started to rain. Though *they* couldn't have gotten any wetter, *we* had managed to stay relatively dry up until then.) We stripped the children down to their underwear and popped them into the car, still squealing with delight. Back home, we streaked into the house, headed straight for the bathtub and dry clothes, then made warm drinks and biscuits and had "tea" by candlelight (the children's idea). It was a wonderful ending, for all of us, to one of the best and most memorable adventures ever.

There were two lessons here for me. As parents, we can be thoughtful about choosing the time and place for messy play, minimizing the hardship on us while not detracting from our children's pleasure. And we can be of use to each other. Just having another adult there made everything seem more possible. I felt stronger, more resilient, more flexible, more tolerant, more loving even. I was leaning on my friend, he was leaning on me— and rather than the drag of dependence, both of us felt only the great gift of support.

7

Cultivating a Wider View

Let the sense of kinship inspire us to unceasing efforts toward a social order free of violence and oppression.

Sounding reasonable and real justice

A well-behaved young lady of nine was playing with her younger brother and cousins. She had choreographed a game of tag — which everyone was enthusiastic about — and announced that the youngest two would be "it." Her brother exploded in frustration. He stomped and cried and yelled that it was unfair. She was gently and firmly insistent; he continued to scream refusal. After a few minutes, she came in to announce sadly that they couldn't play the game because her brother just wouldn't cooperate.

On the face of it, she was right. The game wasn't working — and her brother certainly looked and acted like the problem. But, having a passionate and sturdy little second child of my own, I was aware of another possible point of view. The older sibling, as usual, was making the rules. Once again, he was expected to run his fat little legs off in vain trying to tag the older ones. He couldn't win an argument about it because arguing was another thing she was better at. The only choices he saw were to give up and do it her way — once again — or to resist. And the only way he knew how to resist was to yell.

If only he'd been able to walk calmly into the room and announce sorrowfully that the game was ruined for everyone because *she* refused to be "it." But he couldn't. So she got an incredible edge in winning the adults to her point of view — because she *sounded* like an adult. She was calm and reasonable. She stated the situation in clear, logical form. Adults like being around people who sound calm and reasonable. We are in sympathy with them just on the basis of their tone of voice.

But tone of voice has nothing to do with justice. In this case his grievance was exactly the same as hers. It should have carried exactly the same weight. In another situation, it might have been much stronger, no matter how deeply obscured by tears, rage and flailing of arms.

It seems universally true that those with more power at their command—fuller use of language, longer legs, access to resources or the ear of authorities—are the ones who can most afford to sound reasonable. They have played the larger role in shaping the status quo, establishing ground rules that work to their benefit, and being seen as upholders of rules and order.

It's the ones with less power—less sophisticated language, shorter legs, less access to resources and decision-making—who end up raging and railing against the status quo. This dynamic plays out on many levels: younger children in relation to older ones, all children in relation to adults, marginal members of the society in relation to the establishment.

Of course, loudness and rage are no automatic indication of having justice on one's side. But the next time I hear a reasonable-sounding "adult" position, in conflict with an incoherent bundle of protest, I hope I won't jump to any conclusions. I hope I remember that little brother who had such a legitimate complaint—and listen very carefully to the side that's harder to hear.

A child's eye view of cheating

We were a motley crew, ages three to forty, playing a pick-up game of baseball on vacation. The six-year-old was pretty new to the game, but able to pick up on the rules, understand how to win, and realize how undeveloped his skills were. He was very pleased to be included and wanted to make a solid contribution to his team. We had to bend some rules by necessity, and the tone was a lighthearted one. Noticing the flexibility, he got excited about the possibilities of cheating as his way of helping out. So, as first baseman, he took advantage of a long at-bat to move the rock that was first base off into the bushes. Nobody could get to first base now! Then, as catcher, he started to sneak up and grab the bat from the batter's hand (with all of us cooperating by being obtusely unable to figure out what was going on), then delightedly stepping up to the plate himself and swinging three strikes to give the other team an out. It was an unorthodox game on all counts, and everyone had a great time.

What if we thought about such cheating not as an offense to righteousness, but as a way of helping to equalize power relationships? Especially in structured games with rules, people who are older, more informed, and more experienced invariably have an edge. Young children's cheating can be a very successful way of evening the odds.

If I can take away the moral judgment, and give up some of my attachment to the way the game is *supposed* to be played, it can be a lot of fun. The children get a gleam in their eye and start to cheat, more or less obviously, depending on their level of sophistication. They steal money from the bank (or bases from the playing field), move their player extra spaces, turn the dice, tackle the basketball player just as he is about to shoot, put down three cards at a time. I let them know that I know the game they're really playing (who wants to perform tricks without an audience?), making a great show of helpless outrage. If I try cheating, I have to be less competent at it, or be caught by the child and required to play the game "right." In any case, my role is to protest loudly and helplessly, while they laugh and laugh—secure in the position of greater power. It's the deliciousness of the role reversal that's the whole fun of the game.

I don't think that by playing these games we need to worry about turning our children into cheaters. Some people may become compulsive cheaters, addicted to winning at any cost, but not through such play. Most children know when cheating makes a game fun, and when it just takes away all the structure that allows the game to work well. Even the three-year-olds, who delight in cheating with adults, will work out the rules of a game very carefully with each other. And as they gain information and experience, the challenge of playing by established rules will become more interesting.

What are our goals anyway? I want to raise children who know how to play by the rules, and are secure enough in themselves that they don't have to win every game. But I also want them to realize that the rules of the game are often made by people with more power — people who don't necessarily have our needs or best interests in mind. I want to raise children who are not afraid of challenging rules that never allow them to win.

Finding our way through mass culture

Living in the USA in these times, it's virtually impossible to avoid mass culture. Through TV, movies, video, radio, books, newspapers, toys, comic books, billboards and more, we are pounded with messages that glorify consumerism, reinforce sexual stereotypes, and trivialize and homogenize anything that will turn a buck. We literally breathe in myths about beauty, success, money, sex, violence, power, happiness, good, and evil.

Few of us like the distorted sense of life that mass culture promotes. It's particularly hard to see our children so susceptible to its distortions and lies. As adults, we are affected by this culture, and may want a product that's the latest thing, but rarely with the single-minded intensity of a child.

In can be hard to know how to talk with our children about those values of mass culture that we find repellent — particularly if the commercialized allure of a particular toy, fashion, or script has already seduced them. Our unprocessed load of disgust can stand in the way of any kind of successful communication.

I've been trying to figure out for years what to do about the junky little plastic toys that come into our house—as birthday gifts, from their friends, even as tokens from us to show that we're flexible on our values about quality playthings—and break on the second day. I HATE them. It's hard at the time to think of anything that I hate more. I hate how cheap and glitzy they look. I hate what they symbolize about the distorted values of our country. I hate how those people don't care what they do to children so long as they can make a profit. I hate how deeply disappointed my child gets over a broken piece of shallow exploitative junk, and how powerless I feel in the face of that deep disappointment.

There's nothing wrong with hating all of this, but what predictably ends up happening is that I take it out on the children. "I can't help it," I say, in a voice loaded with frustration. "It's a piece of JUNK! Of course it broke!" Their grief over having such a wonderful toy broken is now compounded by a mother's totally unfeeling response.

I've only recently begun to figure out how to communicate both my passion and my values in this area without blaming my child or his choices. "It makes me *so mad*," I say. "The people who made up that toy just didn't care at all about how the children would feel when it broke. All they cared about was making a lot of money for themselves. I'm sorry, sweetie; I wish it weren't that way." My feelings haven't changed. My values haven't changed. But I've talked about it in a way that clearly indicates that I'm on the child's side.

The more I'm able to do this, the more information they'll actually be able to take in about how the commercialized culture operates and how they fit into it. This may not change their choices or wants in the present, but it will provide them with a larger context for making sense of their world. Most important, it will enable them to continue to use me as an ally as they try to find their way through this maze of conflicting values.

Competition, self-confidence and fun

My sons came home from their soccer game full of good news. "I think that was our team's best game," said the eight-year-old thoughtfully. "We didn't get nearly as tired in the second half as we've done before. That was the half we scored our goal." "I played great," said the eleven-year-old with enthusiasm. Then he added, as an afterthought, "We lost."

Their response to that game was music to my ears. We can't completely barricade off a world of cut-throat competition, a culture that demands that people be characterized either as winners or as losers. But as parents we *can* have an influence on how our children interact with those values, how much they take them on as their own.

I thought of all the different things we've tried. When we play card games, we note the winner (or winners) of each round, but don't keep an overall score. (And a favorite game is one that penalizes you for getting *more* than your bid as well as less, which turns the traditional assumption of winning on its head.) It's easy to take the competition out of party games— answering the questions in a group, playing without the board, doing charades without teams or scores. We've found a couple of wonderful cooperative board games, and are very loose with the rules of competitive ones, feeling free to change them— drastically and in mid-stream if necessary—in order to ensure that everybody has a good time.

When my children started dabbling in team sports, however, I was apprehensive. I wasn't sure that I could stand against the overwhelming pressure of competition that seems inherent in that milieu, where the first question that comes to anyone's lips after a game is "Who won?" I felt very lucky that my son's first coach really emphasized trying hard and having fun more than the score, and I tried to do the same. It was quite a challenge. I remember asking my son how a game had gone. When he said it was fine, I asked if he'd had any good plays, and he told me about them. When he seemed content with that report, I realized that *I* was the one who couldn't feel complete without knowing the score.

There is certainly something to be said for the desire to pursue excellence, to strive to improve, to not be satisfied with comfort or mediocrity. I remember being told about a Chinese ping-pong team when they were unsurpassed in the world. Their strategy, according to this story, was to try and place the ball exactly where the opposing player had to play right at the edge of his competence in order to return it. Although they might win all the games, they were actively challenging themselves, while offering a thoughtful challenge to others. On a simpler scale, in the obstacle courses the children like to organize at their birthday parties, we use a stopwatch; each child is told their own time—and challenged to beat in on the second round.

Although the culture doesn't make it easy, my children are offering me heartening confirmation of the belief that we can strive for excellence at nobody's expense. We can figure out what we need to do to become winners in all aspects of life—and eliminate the category of losers altogether.

Growing up in a divided society

Each time I see black and white toddlers hugging each other, a four-year-old of one color gently touching the face of a baby of another, a mixed group of school-aged children playing raucously together, or teenagers deep in absorbing conversation—each time I feel that I've been given a gift of hope for the future. It seems so natural, so right that they should be together that way. Yet the challenge of raising children who are relaxed, loving, welcoming and confident with each other, in a society where injustice and divisions on the basis of race, class, religion and ethnicity are rampant, is one of the biggest that parents face. As I watch my children growing up, I wonder if, despite my best efforts, they have figured out that some people are not "their kind of people."

What can we do? I think the first step is to realize that even the best intentions cannot protect our children from absorbing the norms of society. It's been helpful to me to think of racism — and others "isms" — as a social poison. It's in the air. We live and breathe it. It's bad for all of us, regardless of our color. Though we can make choices about how we respond, it's not our fault that we are affected by it.

Our children are affected as well. They will pick up things that they see and hear, and try to figure them out, using their most trusted informants to get as complete a picture as they can of the situation. If we're in good communication they will bring us all the questions, stereotypes, and misinformation they hear, in an attempt to get it straightened out in their minds. Sometimes this is very straightforward: "Mommy, why is Jamie's skin a different color?" Other times they will repeat things that they've heard, or act out things that they've seen, as a way of asking for help with them. This is often more difficult for us, since our urge may be to keep them from behaving inappropriately. Yet a response of, "That's not nice," or "I don't ever want to hear you use that word again," just drives the issue underground.

If we can manage to not sound horrified, but simply ask about the context in which they heard or saw that behavior, chances are that we'll open up a way to help them deal with the hurts and confusions of growing up in a world where relations between different groups are not yet right.

One of the most useful things we can do is provide good information about and access to a wide variety of people. We can think about these issues as we make choices about children's books, gifts, where to live and where to visit, friends, childcare, who we invite to dinner, the music we play, the shows we watch. As our children have more and more opportunities to see and hear about the lives of people in different situations, their perspective on the world will broaden and they will have an increasingly solid basis for figuring out the hard spots.

Our children watch us so closely, they count on us so much. If they see us appreciating and respecting the diversity of people in our world; if they see us being friends; if they see us acting against injustice; and if they feel free to come to us with their questions and hurts about growing up in the midst of division and injustice, then they will be well positioned both to live rich lives of their own and to add their weight to the momentum for change.

8

Cultivating Inclusion

Every human being is a child of God with a measure of God's light.

Loving the bully

It was early on a Saturday morning. I was facing a long day alone with the children, and they were squabbling already. Just the thought of what our day could be like made me tired. The older one grabbed a toy eagle away from his brother, claiming ownership. The younger one started to complain loudly, knowing that grabbing out of another person's hands is frowned upon in our family. I restored the eagle, hoping for enough peace to finish my breakfast. The older one could be wonderfully thoughtful, kind and generous in social situations with his peers, and I was counting on those qualities to come through. They didn't. He snatched again and his brother burst into tears.

I knew that the obvious response—demanding different behavior of my firstborn—might produce momentary relief, but was not going to make my day, his, or his brother's go better. Something was going on for him that couldn't be handled by appeals to his best thinking. I could have sent the conflict underground by coercion—which I've done many times before, in that tone of tired irritation that I'm sure most parents know well. But the prospect of having whatever-it-was pop back up in different forms all day long felt even more exhausting than my current tiredness. So I reached for the energy to try something different.

Restoring the eagle to my youngest again, I picked his big brother up and moved us all to the front room, where a carpet and soft chair always make a conflict feel easier to handle.

Holding him in my arms, I tried not to communicate too much annoyance, and he must have picked up my willingness to look for a genuinely good solution. He started playing a "sneak out of my arms" game, which we'd played before. I feigned inattention and let him sneak, but always grabbed him back before he could get to his brother. After a few minutes of laughing/wrestling/ gymnastics/keep-away, he lost all interest in the eagle. His brother played with it in delight and total absorption for a few more minutes, then decided that our game looked like even more fun.

He dropped the eagle and demanded to have a turn. I tried to accommodate them both (not too successfully) and when they ended up squabbling over me, I turned it into a general wrestling session, until their tone with each other indicated that good relations had been restored. They moved easily into some other activity and I went back to the kitchen to finish breakfast and the dishes.

It wasn't a perfect day from then on. We had other fights, in other combinations. But I wasn't inwardly seething, or outwardly erupting, the whole time, and the success of that intervention stayed with me. Rather than doing the obvious — comforting the hurt child and scolding the bully — I had tried a different way. I directed my love and attention to the *bully*, knowing that something hard must have been going on for him to make him act that way. I used my adult power to keep him from further abusing his brother. (It can't be good for anybody to be left alone to abuse another human being.) But rather than judging or condemning, I stayed close and gave him plenty of time to vent whatever it was that weighed on him. And going with that hunch ended up changing the dynamics much more thoroughly than any scolding could possibly have done. We all ended up winners.

Mothers of sons and male culture

One of the puzzles of being a woman raising young men has been how to interact with the male culture that they inhabit—more and more as they grow older. In the beginning it was pretty simple. Who wouldn't choose to roughhouse with a wonderful two-year-old? And if the power of their attraction to trucks and balls was uncanny, they were as charming at that play as they were with the occasional doll and cooking project.

As they got older, however, there were more and more things that I was less and less inclined to do with them. War games were the hardest. These come in all varieties—card, board, computer, video, action figure, little soldier. But the basic premises are the same: how to attack in order to survive, and be smart about who you sacrifice (and when and where) so that you'll come out on top. I just don't like to play that way. To make it worse, while I don't dislike sports, they were not part of my childhood experience, and I don't jump at the opportunity to join in. Their father enjoys both these types of activities, and we've slipped into a pattern where he does those things with the boys, and I participate in an ever-diminishing part of their play life.

It's not the worst thing in the world. They count on me for other things. They know I love them and they love me. I'm not worried that they'll grow up to be war mongers or cut-throat competitive jocks. It's wonderful that they have so much of their father. But still, something hasn't been sitting right with me.

I've been assuming that it makes sense for the men to handle the "male culture" part of our sons' upbringing. Clearly, they're more comfortable with it. Playing those games and going by those rules doesn't seem to bother them. In fact, they seem to enjoy it. Surely I, who have feelings up to my eyeballs about casual violence, preemptive strikes, loss of thousands of lives, and winning-at-any-cost, should step back and let somebody who has a little more slack interact with them in these moments, right? After all, I'm just likely to make harsh judgments—or burst into tears.

I'm coming to think, however, that this assumption is flawed, which raises a very unsettling—and exciting—prospect. What if we women *are the ones* to help our sons with male culture? What if men's comfort with these ways of playing comes not from greater understanding or flexibility, but from their own total immersion in that culture and those values? Perhaps it's all they've ever known.

But if you're inside something, you can't see it very clearly. As women, we have the advantage of seeing from the outside. The intensity of the competition, the willingness to sacrifice guys right and left in order to win, *doesn't* look normal to us. Some of us hate it with a passion. But the fact that we can see it, and name it as a perspective that doesn't nurture the human spirit, positions us to lead the way out.

I think it's important here to appreciate the men in our lives. They never chose to be trained this way. They deserve only praise for every bit of humanity they've retained in the face of an oppressive requirement that they be independent at any cost, in conflict with others to survive, and ultimately expendable. Our men are treasures, their presence in their children's lives is a gift—*and* we can lead the way here. (And perhaps they can help out with the parts of female culture that envelop and blind *us*—and our daughters.)

The details of *how* we actually lead are not entirely clear to me. My guess is that many of us have to start by noticing how intensely we hate some things, and taking space away from our sons to clear out some of those feelings. Once I'm not so filled to overflowing with raw hatred and grief for a system that makes sweet little boys sacrifice their guys and squash their friends in the name of fun, I'll have a little more space to think.

My guess is that it won't be easy, that it will involve stretching in areas where we don't feel competent, trying out things we wouldn't normally choose, trusting that people can make good contact in ways that are totally outside our experience, and taking the time to pour out our anger and grief again and again. I'm sure that it will involve being close, not making judgments, putting out a different point of view, joking around, trying lots of different things, loving the men in our lives, never giving up. And I think everyone will win.

Equal time for girls

What to do about the action figures, the violent play, the aggressive little boys? As I hang out more with early childhood educators, I get an earful of concern about these issues. Now, don't get me wrong. I think they are real and important. The messages directed at little boys from all directions in the culture—that we are the good guys and the bad guys must be destroyed, that the way to solve every problem is by fighting, that violent conflict is fun and exciting and glamorous (and totally lacking in negative consequence)—are scary. Of course our little boys play them out, and of course thoughtful adult intervention is needed, both to help them with their play, and to challenge those messages at their source.

What makes me mad is how that concern can slip into a perspective that sees the little boys as the problematical ones. A preschool teacher, writing about the (real) problems of violent play in the classroom, began generalizing to "wild and aggressive" play, which then generalized to play with lots of "running and shouting." Now preschool classrooms may not be set up to handle "running and shouting" play very well, but it's certainly an intrinsic and positive part of any childhood experience. It's good that little boys know they want to run and shout. Running and shouting play could be fun for all of us.

And it makes me mad that nobody is talking about the girls. Little girls are bombarded with cultural messages just as pervasively as little boys are. While they are learning to kick and destroy, the girls are learning make-up and fashion and romance and the necessity of being attractive to succeed at life. And they play out those messages just as little boys do. They just don't make as much noise about it.

So little girls are perceived as non-problematic. They don't disrupt the classroom. There is no campaign that I'm aware of to get "little girls" toys that are heavy on romance and sexual innuendo off the shelves. Little girls doing make-up in a corner get positive feedback for cooperative behavior (if they're not simply ignored) while little boys doing ninja kicks in the center get pointed out and agonized over.

What if we saw little girls' endless beauty/romance play as a problem equal to little boys' endless war play? What if we felt it just as necessary to put lots of energy into thinking out ways of intervening and offering alternative possibilities? What if we were as worried about little girls who seem unable to run and shout as we are about little boys who seem unable to sit still?

After all, this is a new century. I say, let's not stop thinking about the boys, but let's give the little girls equal time. It's only fair.

Assuming our welcome

A friend of mine has a daughter with a severe genetic disability. She doesn't talk, is awkward in her movements, and is very shy around strangers. Though I've wanted to have a relationship, I don't get to see her often and I, in turn, have been very shy around her.

She doesn't respond quickly to a warm or playful overture. She doesn't say welcoming things. Without convenient verbal cues, and always conscious that her brain is working in a way I don't understand, I become self-conscious in my interactions. Is my greeting welcome? Am I being too persistent, not respecting her desire to be left alone? Am I being condescending? Alternatively, am I trying to relate at a level she can't understand? Not knowing the answer to any of these questions, and not wanting to be disrespectful, I've been inclined to hold back.

I haven't been pleased with this state of affairs. After all, she is the beloved daughter of a dear friend. When the attempt to be respectful in such a situation results in a withdrawal of human contact, *something* is not right.

Another friend offered the vital shift in perspective. She was talking about children with special needs, and commented about what a gift they offer to the people in their lives. Since trying to love them for what they *do* would be an exercise in frustration much of the time, we have to love them just for who they *are*. And loving *them* in this way helps us to remember to love others just for who *they* are—which is what we all want anyway.

Somehow, hearing her say this, I felt permission to love this child—and everything fell into place. When you love a child, you don't worry about how you look, or how they respond. Since most people don't object to being loved, you don't worry about imposing. Verbal cues become unnecessary. You're not dancing some kind of complicated partner dance. You're just offering them your love.

The last time I saw this girl was pure pleasure. I assumed that we were old friends. After all, we both loved her dad, and even though we'd both been shy, we'd spent time together almost monthly for the past year, and that had to count for something. I assumed that a big hug was in order. I assumed that she would be happy to have me snuggle up to her. I assumed that it would be okay to initiate playful games. I assumed that my presence, my love, was welcome.

What a difference! She was obviously pleased, and I felt wonderful. It was like reaching the end of a long journey in foreign lands, no longer trying hard all the time to learn foreign customs and do the right thing so as not to offend. It was like coming home.

It makes me wonder how often, when faced with someone we know is different, we get shy and withhold our natural warmth for fear of doing the wrong thing. How often do children with special needs (and so many others) suffer, and get excluded from our circle of warmth because of this diffidence? What would it be like if we always assumed that our love was welcome?

Claiming all our children

Whenever we go away on vacation, I wonder why I live in the city. The children soak up the open spaces and revel in each new adventure. We have slow days, full of nature. Friends who have built their lives around rural farms ask if the city is as dreadful as the news makes it sound, with all the talk of danger and drugs and financial insolvency. When they declare that they would never live in the city, I don't know what to say. We come back to the heat and noise, shorter tempers and too much to do and, as always, I feel a little jealous — and I wonder if I've made a big mistake.

Of course vacation is always different from daily life, but the contrast is startling. Along with the oppressive heat and the backlog of work, this time we came home to the possibility of becoming foster parents to the grandson of a dear friend, his mother having gotten lost on cocaine. Unexpectedly, this little boy, a symbol of all that is wrong with the city, becomes a means of noticing all that is right. We don't know if our lives can stretch wide enough to include him, but there is something in us that is willing to try. He is one of the children of our city. He is one of us.

It turns out that his mother finds a rehab program that will include children. We're relieved. It's a much better solution. But having a chance to cry for this little boy, and to notice our willingness to be part of his life, I can see what I value most about living here.

I love the city for many reasons. I love all the cultural

resources. I love being able to walk to the drugstore, preschool, corner grocery, friends' houses. I love all our proud history. I love the old architecture. But most of all I love being so unlimited in who I can claim as my people.

I love driving—or walking or biking—the streets of our neighborhood and noticing that I can never predict the color of the next person I'll see. I love having the children experience this as normal. It's just a part of our everyday lives.

Black, white and Vietnamese boys work together, fixing a bike on a neighbor's porch. My children answer the doorbell, and it's an older black boy wanting to borrow the basketball. They know it's safe to lend, that it will be returned. My husband, our Chinese tenant and a batch of teenagers of all races go out to play ball together. We go sledding in the park, share sleds as always, and the children come home with a new friend, one they might never have met in another context.

I think of my friends who live with open spaces, beautiful horizons, big gardens, and a buffer from street crime. I know that many of the things that are most wrong in society get concentrated in our cities. It's a struggle to figure out how best to be part of the solution. But this time, I don't feel jealous. There is much to value and love about the country but being here in this city, in this neighborhood, I get to have something that I would never give up. I get to claim all our children.

About the author

Pamela Haines is a long-time resident of West Philadelphia with a passion for the earth, for economic integrity, and for right relationship. Her paid work is in childcare including leadership capacity and community building and organizing for policy change; she also teaches peer counseling and leads family play groups.

She is active in her Quaker community, in urban agriculture, and in environmental and economic justice work. She has led a variety of workshops on faith, economics and investment, and has spoken on the topics of finance, climate, justice and racism.

She has deep connections with indigenous communities in Canada and Northern Uganda, provides ongoing emotional support to a handful of young climate activist leaders, and is happily engaged in the lives of her local grandchildren. At home, she loves quilting and repair of all kinds, and blogs at www.pamelalivinginthisworld.blogspot.com.

Previous titles

Toward a Right Relationship with Finance: Interest, Debt, Growth and Security
This book offers background on our current economic system within the context of our deepest values and beliefs; suggests plausible alternatives to that system, particularly with regard to financing retirement; and invites the reader to imagine new forms of durable economic and social security in a transformed and life-centered economy.

Waging Peace: Discipline and Practice
This pamphlet offers a window into how to become nonviolent warriors as we learn to hope, grieve, listen, welcome conflict, mend, speak truth and cultivate courage. Engaging stories bring

these practices to life and show that by working together we can transform ourselves, our community, and our world.

Money and Soul: Quaker Faith and Practice and the Economy
For anyone who takes seriously the challenge of bringing our faith into the world, knotty issues around economics crop up at every turn, especially if we are willing to ask the big questions: What is the economy for? How much is enough? What needs to be equal? How is well-being best measured? Who should decide?

Alive in This World
The poems in this collection combine close observation of life — in all its forms — with a deep commitment to justice. They offer vivid images, make sometimes surprising connections, and leave the reader grounded in the goodness of being alive.

That Clear and Certain Sound: Finding Solid Ground in Perilous Times
This collection of meditations on being alive in these wonderful and perilous times encourages us to stay alert to the sound of truth even in the most unlikely places, to reach for solid ground in all aspects of our lives, and to stretch from there toward lives of greater connection and integrity.

From the Author

Thank you for purchasing *Tending Sacred Ground: Respectful Parenting*. My sincere hope is that you derived as much from reading this book as I have in creating it. If you have a few moments, please feel free to add your review of the book to your favorite online site for feedback. Also, if you would like to connect with me and my ongoing work, please visit my website or social media page, or go to my blog: www.pamelalivinginthisworld.blogspot.com

Sincerely,

Pamela Haines

CHRISTIAN ALTERNATIVE
BOOKS

THE NEW OPEN SPACES

Throughout the two thousand years of Christian tradition there
have been, and still are, groups and individuals that exist in
the margins and upon the edge of faith. But in Christianity's
contrapuntal history it has often been these outcasts and
pioneers that have forged contemporary orthodoxy out
of former radicalism as belief evolves to engage with and
encompass the ever-changing social and scientific realities. Real
faith lies not in the comfortable certainties of the Orthodox,
but somewhere in a half-glimpsed hinterland on the dirt track
to Emmaus, where the Death of God meets the Resurrection,
where the supernatural Christ meets the historical Jesus,
and where the revolution liberates both the oppressed and
the oppressors.

Welcome to Christian Alternative... a space at the edge where
the light shines through.
If you have enjoyed this book, why not tell other readers by
posting a review on your preferred book site.

Recent bestsellers from Christian Alternative are:

Bread Not Stones
The Autobiography of An Eventful Life
Una Kroll
The spiritual autobiography of a truly remarkable woman
and a history of the struggle for ordination in the Church of
England.
Paperback: 978-1-78279-804-0 ebook: 978-1-78279-805-7

The Quaker Way
A Rediscovery
Rex Ambler
Although fairly well known, Quakerism is not well understood.
The purpose of this book is to explain how Quakerism works as
a spiritual practice.
Paperback: 978-1-78099-657-8 ebook: 978-1-78099-658-5

Blue Sky God
The Evolution of Science and Christianity
Don MacGregor
Quantum consciousness, morphic fields and blue-sky
thinking about God and Jesus the Christ.
Paperback: 978-1-84694-937-1 ebook: 978-1-84694-938-8

Celtic Wheel of the Year
Tess Ward
An original and inspiring selection of prayers combining
Christian and Celtic Pagan traditions, and interweaving their
calendars into a single pattern of prayer for every morning
and night of the year.
Paperback: 978-1-90504-795-6

Christian Atheist

Belonging without Believing

Brian Mountford

Christian Atheists don't believe in God but miss him: especially the transcendent beauty of his music, language, ethics, and community.

Paperback: 978-1-84694-439-0 ebook: 978-1-84694-929-6

Compassion Or Apocalypse?

A Comprehensible Guide to the Thoughts of René Girard

James Warren

How René Girard changes the way we think about God and the Bible, and its relevance for our apocalypse-threatened world.

Paperback: 978-1-78279-073-0 ebook: 978-1-78279-072-3

Diary Of A Gay Priest

The Tightrope Walker

Rev. Dr. Malcolm Johnson

Full of anecdotes and amusing stories, but the Church is still a dangerous place for a gay priest.

Paperback: 978-1-78279-002-0 ebook: 978-1-78099-999-9

Do You Need God?

Exploring Different Paths to Spirituality Even For Atheists

Rory J.Q. Barnes

An unbiased guide to the building blocks of spiritual belief.

Paperback: 978-1-78279-380-9 ebook: 978-1-78279-379-3

Readers of ebooks can buy or view any of these bestsellers by clicking on the live link in the title. Most titles are published in paperback and as an ebook. Paperbacks are available in traditional bookshops. Both print and ebook formats are available online.

Find more titles and sign up to our readers' newsletter at
http://www.johnhuntpublishing.com/christianity
Follow us on Facebook at
https://www.facebook.com/ChristianAlternative